HITLER'S
PROPHECY

HITLER'S PROPHECY

The Key to the Holocaust

SIMON BURGESS

VALLENTINE MITCHELL
LONDON • CHICAGO

First published in 2022 by Vallentine Mitchell

Catalyst House,
720 Centennial Court,
Centennial Park, Elstree WD6 3SY, UK

814 N. Franklin Street,
Chicago, Illinois,
60610 USA

www.vmbooks.com

Copyright © 2022 Simon Burgess

British Library Cataloguing in Publication Data:
An entry can be found on request

ISBN 978 1 912676 97 2 (Paper)
ISBN 978 1 912676 98 9 (Ebook)

Library of Congress Cataloging in Publication Data:
An entry can be found on request

Contents

Acknowledgements

Excerpts from official documents are reprinted with the consent of the National Archives, Kew, London. The following libraries and archives have kindly provided valuable material: the British Library and in particular the Newsroom, London; the British Library of Political and Economic Science, London; the German Historical Institute, London; the Wellcome Institute, London; the Wiener Library, London; the Institut für Stadtgeschichte, Mannheim, Germany; the Kungliga Biblioteket, Stockholm, Sweden; the Malmö Stadsarkiv (and Anette Sarnäs); the United States National Archives; and the Hoover Institution Library (with the research assistance of Jenny Fichmann). I am also grateful to Professor Dan Michman for his very helpful suggestions. Thanks are due to CriticalPast for permission to use the front cover photograph.

Introduction
The Final Problem

'Hitler's will', British intelligence reported in December 1945, 'has been discovered'.[1] It was found sewn into the shoulder padding of a German prisoner-of-war during a routine search. The prisoner turned out to be a trusted messenger who had left Hitler's besieged Reich Chancellery bunker in Berlin on 29 April with instructions to try to reach the headquarters in northern Germany of Admiral Doenitz, nominated by Hitler as his successor. The genuineness of the will – in fact a personal will and a political testament – was quite certain. Hitler's signature was authenticated by experts. The text had clearly been prepared using the special *Führer*-typewriter, the large typeface compensating for his weak eyesight. The contents of the will tallied with various accounts about the final few hours in the bunker obtained from interviews with many witnesses.[2] But the clinching factor was the characteristic style. 'His political testament', the intelligence officer wrote:

> ...is divided into two parts, the first being a tirade disclaiming all responsibility for the war and blaming it on the Jews, whom he says were the real agency which led England into war with Germany in 1939. In this he again states that he has no intention of falling into enemy hands, but will instead stay in Berlin and choose death voluntarily at the moment when he feels his position can no longer be maintained. He orders, however, the rest of the German people to continue fighting with all possible means. The whole document is full of the type of phrase which occurred so frequently in his speeches. It is perhaps significant that the last words he writes in his will are 'International Jewry', which sufficiently indicates the state of his mind at the time.[3]

Because the will explicitly specified that Hitler had decided to take his own life, the British hoped that publication would finally dispose of the idea, circulating for several months since VE (Victory in Europe) Day, that Hitler was still alive. The will was, in addition, thought likely to be of considerable interest to 'the future historian'. For the time being officials felt it would be best to consult first with other Allied governments. In the event, when a British team tracked down a second copy of the will (along with Hitler's marriage contract with Eva Braun) in Bavaria, in the American-administered zone, the local US army commander called a press conference to make public the news. This then prompted the release of lengthy extracts, including some of the more sensational passages translated from the testament.

The message the testament contained was, on the face of it, unambiguous. It was untrue, Hitler proclaimed, that he or anybody else in Germany had 'wanted war' in 1939. He regretted that 'after the first terrible world war a second war should arise'. It was entirely the fault of 'those international statesmen who were either of Jewish origin or worked in Jewish interests' who had 'designed' and 'provoked' it. For that reason he had, he said, 'left no doubt' that 'the real culprit in this murderous struggle, Jewry, would also have to pay for it. I also [he emphasised] left no doubt that it would not be tolerated this time that millions of European children of Aryan people should be starved to death, that millions of men should die, and that hundreds of thousands of women and children should be burned and bombed to death in their cities without the real culprit suffering due punishment, even though by more humane methods.'[4]

That 24 leading Nazis were on trial in Nuremberg added to the timeliness of the publication. The German press had lately been full of shocking tales about the 'senseless destruction' inflicted on the huge number of Jews who were missing or unaccounted for. Excerpts from the will, at least in Germany, were largely quoted without comment. Coverage in the rest of Europe and beyond was far more forthright. Hitler's testament was widely viewed as a 'confession', an attempt to justify the horrors that were now coming to light, 'a last alibi' excusing the ferocity of his 'war of vengeance'. Addressing the German nation, Germany's conquerors and posterity, he was 'revealing' – one weekly magazine wrote – 'that he, personally, ordered the "humane" extermination of 6,000,000 European Jews'.[5]

Hermann Goering, one of the highest-ranking among the accused, tried to deny that the testament was 'proof' of anything. Hitler must have had 'a definite understanding' with Heinrich Himmler, the *Reichsführer* of the *Schutzstaffel* (or SS), otherwise the magnitude of the outrages 'would have been impossible', but Hitler 'just left things' to Himmler, whose 'chosen psychopaths' carried it all out, while 'it was kept secret from the rest of us'. Hitler, Goering alleged, only took responsibility at the very end.[6] Unsurprisingly Goering and several of his fellow defendants used this line of argument to maintain their innocence, insisting they had had no knowledge of or involvement in any antisemitic acts. One defence lawyer even made use of the testament in open court, stating that the 'slaughter' of the Jews was 'in atonement' for the death of so many Germans, a 'reprisal' measure that his client was wrongly being charged with. Only Hans Frank, the former Governor-General of occupied Poland, fully owned up. 'In contrast to other people around the *Führer* who seemed to know nothing, I did know what was going on', he accepted. Everything was done on Hitler's 'direct command'. In his will Hitler was 'attesting to the most horrible crime in world history'.[7]

There was, at this early stage, some awareness that in the midst of so much persecution, enslavement and annihilation of defenceless civilians, Hitler's regime had been engaged in the 'genocide' (a newly-coined term) of an entire people. But the legalistic grounds for guilt were largely based on complicity rather than direct participation. What investigators lacked was an overall sense of the decision-making that had gone on. The principal villains – Hitler, Himmler and Joseph Goebbels, Minister for Propaganda – were dead. An immense archive was captured, but in the closing weeks of the war many thousands of the most sensitive files had been deliberately burnt. The main extermination camps no longer existed. Agile defendants like Goering ran rings round their interrogators. A written *Führerbefehl* ordering the end of European Jewry could not be found. In the absence of a paper trail, it was a struggle to explain 'the deepest enigma of all – just when, and for what "reason", did the ruling clique decide to exterminate the Jews?'[8]

The pioneering studies by Leon Poliakov (1951), Gerald Reitlinger (1953), and Raul Hilberg (1961) set out to carefully examine the machinery of murder and the motivation of the murderers.[9] Poliakov, though he recognised that much still remained 'shrouded in darkness', provided a sketch of the programme 'signed' by Hitler, 'the Master', and some of his associates, a plan of action which emerged in stages, by trial and error, and with an increasing tempo as the tide of the Second World War turned against Germany. In Reitlinger's 'ghastly chronicle'[10], he too was persuaded that Hitler had 'started the machine working'. Reitlinger described a convoluted and untidy procedure, left largely to subordinates in an obscure delegation of authority that was unlikely to ever be intelligible. But he had no hesitation in stating that Hitler had at least inspired it. The narrative framework adopted by Hilberg was, by comparison, more methodical, making thorough use of German documentation, and also the most conceptualised. In his version of 'how the deed was done', the persecution of Jewry followed a clear progression of logical steps, originally in Germany and then broadening out to encompass wartime Europe, in a meticulous and orderly exertion of bureaucratic (administrative, military and industrial) power. The tendency was always in an intensifying direction, though the end point – annihilation – was not conceived of in any pre-determined way, not even by Hitler.[11] Allowing for the uncertainty, all three of them believed a commitment to eradicate those Jews within Germany's grasp had been made by the time of the launching of the German attack on the Soviet Union in mid-1941. They also had in common the outlook, as Hugh Trevor-Roper put it in his review of Hilberg, that without Hitler's pathological obsession with the Jewish race there would have been no 'holocaust'.[12]

These individual inquests were unusual, for their time, in treating the war on the Jews as a distinct topic rather than an awkward aspect of the broader history of Hitler's war. It was not until the 1970s that there was a general expansion in scholarly debate about 'the Final Solution' in its own right. Authors began challenging the notion of Hitler's centrality and the 'almost unanimous' assumption of a critical decision prior to the Russian campaign. Uwe Adam identified the slowing down of the German army's advance from September to November 1941 as the decisive phase which had elevated the *Ostkrieg* into an 'all or nothing' contest and induced Hitler to initiate the first exterminationist measures.[13] Developments did not emanate from a preconceived plan. There was a policy mess, with escalating violence by lower-level officials arising in response to logistical dilemmas which the Nazi regime had created for itself. Martin Broszat, in dismissing the suggestion (advanced, after Goering, by David Irving) that Himmler eliminated European Jewry behind Hitler's back, did however think that there probably was no 'single secret order'.[14] Killing was improvised to begin with and was only systematically applied later on. This, he concluded, fitted the sequence of events much better than the 'demonic explanation' of a long-nurtured intent.[15] It also widened the net of responsibility. It did not, he wanted to say, 'exonerate' Hitler. Taking Broszat's argument one stage further, Hans Mommsen made the claim that Hitler had not issued an order either in a written or in a verbal form. Everything unfolded in a series of small steps and individual actions, cloaked in ambiguity, preventing anyone from objecting. Ideology was important, but what really mattered was the anarchic way in which policy was translated into practice.[16]

Emphasis on the structural apparatus did away with some of the more literal-minded interpreting of Hitler's motives, acting as a creative stimulus. If, troublingly, the solving of the 'Jewish question' was not unequivocally ordered, would a redefining of what was meant by an order help to clarify what happened? Christopher Browning, replying to Broszat[17], sidestepped the uninformative contributions of senior Nazis at Nuremberg by recalling the 'credible' disclosures of more junior SS officers who testified about a decisional moment in the late summer of 1941. Buoyed up by the 'euphoria' of military successes on the eastern front, the conceiving of a total plan grew out of the mass shootings already under way in the Baltic and in Ukraine. Examining the coded language of officialdom, Browning demonstrated how the hurry to prepare a scheme 'solicited' and 'handed down' by Hitler accounted for the muddle of false starts and delays. The first really significant measure, the beginning of the deportation of Germany's Jews, began before anyone had worked out how to eliminate them. Hitler did not push a button. He proposed his 'new and awesome task' informally, and this was 'gradually understood', 'unevenly disseminated' and 'slowly implemented'. Using many of the same sources but adding a large amount of fresh material, Gerald Fleming compiled a painstaking report establishing an 'unbroken continuity' from Hitler's adolescence to the 'venomous' last testament, distinguished throughout by an abiding strain of Judeophobia.[18] By hunting down every meaningful utterance and witness statement, Fleming could claim that Hitler's 'commanding' part in 'blotting out' the Jews was abundantly evident, notwithstanding the camouflaging of his role. Himmler was his reluctant intermediary, habitually employing a telling phrase, 'the *Führer's* wish', intended to constitute an instruction that was as binding as an order in writing. In so doing, Hitler pursued his 'sacred aim'.[19]

A further, intriguing redefinition by L.J. Hartog appeared in a short essay and in a later, longer book.[20] Hartog chided the politicians of the 1930s and historians thereafter for failing to take Hitler at his word. Hartog's Hitler was inspired by a self-appointed 'mission' to bring about, initially at any rate, the German domination of Europe. He hoped to achieve this by limiting conflict to the European continent. His arch-enemy – the Jews – stood in his way. To outwit their expected opposition he devised an 'infernal' ruse, threatening that unless Germany's aspirations were met the Jews of Europe would answer for it. They were his bargaining counter to hold off a general, that is to say a world war.[21] When a world war did break out, he destroyed all the Jews he could. The '*Endlösung*' was not something his regime slipped into, almost accidentally. It was a calculated, 'programmed' outcome that would result should his advice be ignored. When the United States entered the war in December 1941, all that remained was for Hitler to 'nod his head'.

Philippe Burrin, coincidentally, had been thinking along similar lines.[22] Scarred by the 'trauma' of Germany's defeat in 1918 and determined to right the wrongs that ensued, Hitler issued a warning laying out his 'conditional' terms. Had his demands for greater 'living space' been accepted, the Jews, though subjected to much misery, would at the worst have been expelled from Europe. By forming a powerful combine of states and denying him what he wanted, the 'Jewish international' was playing with fire. His project foundered, so set he set about eliminating altogether the Jews under German control, avenging the loss of German blood and preventing the reinstating of Jewish power in a defeated Germany. Burrin made a point of saying that things were very much hanging in the balance right up until Hitler's first inkling, in August 1941, that his attack on the Soviet Union was backfiring. Despair, rather than Browning's euphoria, was the psychological frame of mind. At that moment of truth, the order to deport the Jews of Germany was identical, Burrin contended, with their extermination.

Access after 1989 to Soviet and other east European archives led to an even stronger burst in scholarly output, altering the territorial focus. There was a desire, as well, to abandon the acrimonious tone which had, until that point, affected many disputes.[23] Burrin, assessing the historiographical state of play, noted a new balancing of elements of antisemitic ideology, the functioning of the regime and the influence of context; as yet, however, his colleagues had not come up with a convincing analysis of cause and effect.[24] The accuracy of this judgment was illustrated by the lukewarm reception given to the apparent breakthrough made by Christian Gerlach, one of a team of researchers working on the diaries of Goebbels that had turned up in Moscow. Spotting Goebbels's mention of a hitherto unknown Hitler speech in December 1941, Gerlach thought he had identified the very moment when Hitler disclosed 'the decision in principle' to murder all of Europe's Jews. Gerlach's 'ingenious' argument upset just about everyone.[25] Asked for their opinion, most reviewers stuck to their guns, either favouring an earlier date or rejecting what, to them, was the pointless pursuit of the non-existent.

In his biography of Hitler and in several specialist articles, Ian Kershaw formulated an explanatory model reconciling the opposing schools.[26] He made Hitler's 1939 prophecy the key motif, the metaphorical clue linking high politics with the pressures for radical action from below. The unveiling of the prophecy was neither an extravagant announcement nor a propaganda stunt. On notable occasions from early 1941 onwards, both publicly and privately, Hitler repeated his lurid threat. These instances were, according to Kershaw, 'signals' giving a 'green light' to his followers to take further bold steps. He was the 'spur', but they had plenty of leeway in terms of action, allowing him to communicate his intentions without having to spell out what should be done. The timing of this signalling was explored and Kershaw was not unaware of the strategic dimension of 'the blackmail ploy'. On the whole, nevertheless, he ascribed the main thrust of anti-Jewish policy to a 'mutually reinforcing' quest for racial purity. His was a fusion of rival approaches, stressing the ideological impulse but positing an internally impelled, step-wise progression, starting off in the occupied East, extending to the expulsion of Germany's Jews and then, finally, to an all-embracing programme of liquidation. 'There was no single document ordering systematic annihilation', one reviewer commented, 'but at each critical juncture along the road to mass murder, [Kershaw] finds Hitler nodding approval, encouraging initiatives and, at times, pushing out ahead of his genocidal lieutenants'.[27]

Piecing together at some length what the German people were actually told in the press, on the radio, and in mass-produced pamphlets and street posters about the way the war developed, Jeffrey Herf very much concurred. Hitler's prophecy formed the 'core' of the public discourse.[28] It expressed the 'paranoid logic', typical too in Hitler's private discussions with Goebbels, Himmler and others, of an obsessively held world view of Jewish omnipotence. How else, Hitler argued to his own satisfaction after invading Russia, was it possible to explain the incomprehensible overnight alliance of capitalist England and the United States with the communist Soviet Union? Although Herf focused chiefly on the rationale for action rather than the detailed decisional arena, he did observe that in these same weeks, as German forces first engaged in the massacring of Jewish civilians, the 'realising' of Hitler's prophecy began to be publicly broadcast, often in the plainest of wording.

The 'prophecy' thesis has its doubters. The idea that Hitler set a sort of diplomatic trap is regarded as 'speculative'. The things he said at one time or another should never be taken at face value. To suggest an exterminationist aim was adopted mainly because of a foreign policy imperative is wrong-headed, although the Nazis were only too ready to employ it as a cynical pretext to support moves they were going to make anyway. And where is the chapter and verse to back up such a coupling?

The need is not to look at 'categorical pronouncements' but at the precise circumstances when Hitler came to appreciate it was 'easier to kill Jews than to deport them', enabling his global vision to be localised in the 'bloodlands' of eastern Europe.[29] Too much reliance – such sceptics feel – is put on an 'intuitive' narrating of what may have gone on.

This is the central paradox that students must wrestle with. Hitler's Holocaust, once only of secondary interest, is now seen to be a matter of supreme importance. But Hitler's many angry, chilling expressions of hatred, 'intrinsic' to his 'monstrous vision'[30], sit side-by-side with the few, maddeningly vague scraps of official paper that deal directly with the mechanics of death, confounding attempts to go beyond what he said and ascertain what he did or instructed others to do in his name.[31]

As it happens, the digitising and distribution of historical records is revolutionising the study of all areas of modern history, opening up the paper-based, sound and video archives of libraries and archival depositories. This is of subject-specific benefit with Holocaust materials, which are geographically so widely dispersed and often hard to locate or gain access to.[32] Digitised history means that scholars can make full use of newly available primary sources. The online archive comes to their desk, with additional tools such as searchable databases. In the case of one notable example, the website of the Wannsee Haus museum (the venue for the formal discussion by officials of 'the Final Solution of the Jewish Question' in January 1942) features a colour reproduction of the only surviving copy of the Wannsee protocol and a good deal of associated correspondence culled from elsewhere, helpfully uniting and exposing them to forensic scrutiny.[33] But it is also now much easier to piece together, cross-compare and re-evaluate older manuscripts. Many were produced for judicial purposes at Nuremberg and elsewhere, and are usually considered to be a mixed blessing. With any exercise in detection, however, their usefulness can be assisted by their tendentious character, generating novel insights. Both these ways – providing care is taken not to indulge in inductive cherry-picking[34] – offer valuable opportunities to try and bridge the gap between Hitler's words and Hitler's deeds.

Hitler's final fate was quite quickly established in 1945. The story as well of his downfall has been comprehensively retold many times and even cinematically reimagined. Is the long-running altercation about the grotesque boast in his political testament – inflicting upon the Jews of Europe the 'due punishment' he had threatened them with beforehand – now also able to be satisfactorily elucidated?

Notes

1. Draft of a press handout by the Intelligence Group of the Control Commission for Germany (British Zone), on or around 4 December 1945 (The National Archives of the UK, WO 208/3779, p.95). Accessed on 11 November 2020 from: http://discovery.nationalarchives.gov.uk/details/r/C4413346#imageViewerLink.

2. The results of this inquiry were eventually published by the officer who undertook it, Hugh Trevor-Roper, in *The Last Days of Hitler* (London: Macmillan, 1947).

3. WO 208/3779, p.96.

4. *The Manchester Guardian*, 31 December 1945.

5. *La Gazette de Lausanne*, 31 December 1945; *The Argus* (Melbourne), 31 December 1945; *The Sydney Morning Herald*, 1 January 1946; *The Chicago Sentinel*, 5 January 1946.

6. G. Gilbert, *Nuremberg Diary* (New York: Farrar, Straus and Company, 1947), pp.38-9, p.70 and pp.378-9.

7. Gilbert, *ibid*, p.70 and p.277; also L. Goldensohn, *The Nuremberg Interviews* (London: Pimlico, 2006), p.36.

8. M.J. Lasky, 'The First Glimmer of Extermination', in *Commentary*, 1 August 1948.

9. L. Poliakov, *Bréviaire de la Haine – Le IIIe Reich et les Juifs* (Paris: Calmann-Levy, 1951); G. Reitlinger, *The Final Solution* (London: Vallentine, Mitchell, 1953); R. Hilberg, *The Destruction of the European Jews* (Chicago, IL: Quadrangle Books, 1961).

10. Elizabeth Wiskemann reviewing the book in *The Times Literary Supplement*, 1 May 1953.

11. R. Hilberg, *The Politics of Memory* (Chicago, IL: Ivan R. Dee, 1996), pp.63-4.

12. H.Trevor-Roper, 'Nazi Bureaucrats and Jewish Leaders', in *Commentary*, 1 April 1962.

13. U. Adam, *Judenpolitik im Dritten Reich* (Düsseldorf: Droste Verlag, 1972), especially Chapter VII.

14. M. Broszat, 'Hitler und die Genesis der "Endlösung": Aus Anlass der Thesen von David Irving', in *Vierteljahrshefte für Zeitgeschichte*, 25, 4 (October 1977), p.756.

15. See Broszat's comments quoted in *The Sunday Times*, 6 May 1984.

16. H. Mommsen, 'National Socialism – Continuity and Change', in W. Laqueur (ed.), *Fascism: A Reader's Guide: Analyses, Interpretations, Bibliography* (Berkeley and Los Angeles, CA: University of California Press, 1976), pp.179-210; and 'Die Realisierung des Utopischen: Die "Endlösung der Judenfrage" im "Dritten Reich"', in *Geschichte und Gesellschaft*, 9, 3 (1983), pp.381-420.

17. C. Browning, 'Zur Genesis der "Endlösung" – eine Antwort an Martin Broszat', in *Vierteljahrshefte für Zeitgeschichte*, 29, 1 (January 1981), pp.97-109.

18. G. Fleming, *Hitler and the Final Solution* (Berkeley and Los Angeles, CA:University of California Press, 1984).

19. Quoting Saul Friedländer's paper, 'From Anti-Semitism to Extermination' (1984), p.16. Friedländer wrote the Introduction to Fleming's book.

20. *Die Zeit*, 27 January 1989; L.J. Hartog, *Der Befehl zum Judenmord: Hitler, Amerika und die Juden* (Bodenheim: Syndikat,1997)(Dutch edition – *Hoe ontstond de jodenmoord?* (Den Haag: Sdu Uitgeverij Koninginnegracht, 1994).

21. Shlomo Aronson, in a 1984 article, puts it neatly – the more that 'Jewish influence' was used, as Hitler saw it, to bring on a full-scale war, the more the lives of the Jews

collectively would be put at risk ('Die dreifache Falle – Hitlers Judenpolitik, die Allierten und die Juden', in *Vierteljahrshefte für Zeitgeschichte*, 32, 1 (January 1984), pp.29-65).

22.   P. Burrin, *Hitler et les Juifs – Genèse d'un génocide* (Paris: Seuil, 1989).

23.   Browning was notably fair, praising Burrin's research but adding that he remained 'respectfully unconvinced', *The American Historical Review*, 96, 4 (October 1991), p.1226.

24.   P. Burrin, 'Le génocide des juifs en débats', in *Le Monde Diplomatique*, June 1997, p.26.

25.   G. Aly, in the *Berliner Zeitung*, 13 December 1997.

26.   I. Kershaw, *Hitler 1936-1945: Nemesis* (London: Allen Lane, 2000), especially Chapter 10; *Fateful Choices: Ten Decisions that Changed the World, 1940-1941* (London: Allen Lane, 2007), particularly Chapter 10; and 'Hitler's role in the Final Solution' in *Hitler, the Germans and the Final Solution* (Yale, CT: Yale University Press, 2008), pp.89-116.

27.   *The Economist*, 30 September 2000.

28.   J. Herf, *The Jewish Enemy – Nazi Propaganda during World War II and the Holocaust* (Cambridge, MA: Harvard University Press, 2006).

29.   T. Snyder, 'Hitler's inevitable decision?', in *History Today*, 12 December 2015.

30.   I. Kershaw, 'Hitler's Place in History' (Open University lecture, 2005). Accessed on 3 February 2021 from: http://www.open.edu/openlearn/history-the-arts/history/ou-lecture-2005-transcript.

31.   The task as it was explicated in Mr Justice Gray's High Court judgment in the Irving libel trial, reprinted in *The Irving Judgment* (London: Penguin Books, 2000), p.309.

32.   Peter Longerich, who was a member of the defence team in the libel claim brought by David Irving against Penguin Books in 2000, found the drawing together of original documents, spread 'far and wide', a great challenge; in some cases, they had to be faxed to his team while the court proceedings were going on. See *The Unwritten Order – Hitler's Role in the Final Solution* (Stroud: Tempus, 2001), pp.13-4. The EU-funded European Holocaust Research Infrastructure (EHRI) has led the way in building an online platform enabling archival institutions to integrate information about their holdings in a larger network, accessed through a single point of entry.

33.   Accessed on 3 February 2021 from: https://www.ghwk.de/wannsee-konferenz/dokumente-zur-wannsee-konferenz/.

34.   W. Lower, 'The History and Future of Holocaust Research', in *The Tablet*, 26 April 2018. Accessed on 3 February 2021 from: https://www.tabletmag.com/jewish-arts-and-culture/culture-news/260677/history-future-holocaust-research.

1

1918

In the spring of 1918 - the fourth year of what was already being called the Great or World War – the German army launched an immense offensive on the western front, determined to end the military stalemate by punching a hole in the enemy line, splitting apart the British and French forces and propelling the British towards the Channel ports. Using new tactics devised by General Ludendorff, the Germans made large territorial gains. In a series of follow-up operations in the early summer they had advanced to within 60 kilometres of Paris. Having fought Russia into submission, Germany and its Austro-Hungarian ally appeared to be on the verge of a final, decisive victory. In a matter of weeks, however, this expectation was rudely shattered. The British and French, reinforced by the arrival of the first American troops, successfully counterattacked. The retreating Germans were hustled and harried as far as the Belgian border. The German Chief of Staff, Field Marshal Hindenburg, acutely aware he had all but exhausted his remaining reserves, urgently pressed Kaiser Wilhelm to sue for peace. At the start of November the Kaiser himself was persuaded to abdicate. A civilian government was hurriedly formed and the country hovered on the brink of anarchy. From one moment to the next, Germany had collapsed. How, bewildered Germans asked, had this sudden, complete catastrophe come about?

One explanation was actively promoted from the off in nationalist circles. Because Germany's armed forces had not really been beaten on the field of battle (the generals having left it to the politicians to sign an armistice), honour was intact. Germany had only given up owing to internal unrest at home, fomented by strikers and defeatists who undermined the country's fighting capacity and weakened the popular will. The army, in the words supposedly suggested by a British officer to Ludendorff and then popularised by Hindenburg, had been 'stabbed in the back.'[1]

This version of events, though fraudulent[2], had a powerful emotional appeal. The Imperial German Army was entirely exonerated, the blame shifting instead to the disgraceful behaviour of cowardly deserters, pacifist agitators disseminating bogus enemy promises of a just settlement and 'red' radicals infected by 'the bacillus of Asiatic socialism' emanating from the ongoing mayhem in Russia. A particular grumble of the right-wing press was 'the debilitating activity of Jews.'[3] Germany, confronted by 'mortal enemies' committed to destroying the German nation, had been undone from within by a conspiracy of 'foreigners' and 'cosmopolitans.' The perpetrators should have been sent to the front, or put in a labour camp, or – better still – 'strung up'. Many who ought to 'blush with shame', it was noted, were renowned figures in the new democratic republic.

The importance of the 'stab in the back' idea was that it was not just a momentary grievance. It became the basis of a violent call for revenge, to undo recent humiliations and punish those held to have been at fault. Germany had not lost militarily, only politically. 'The day will come', the conservative daily *Die Kreuzzeitung* wrote, 'when the political Messiah we have been lacking in this war will rise up' and German pride will be 'restored'.[4]

Several ultrapatriotic movements flourished in the post-war period, loudly denouncing the Treaty of Versailles as an Anglo-Saxon swindle and exploiting economic instability in order to chip away at the legitimacy of the Weimar regime. The small National Socialist German Workers' Party, centred in Munich, initially attracted attention in 1922 when its leader, Adolf Hitler, part-war veteran and part-street activist, began, despite much ridiculing by leftists[5], to build a reputation as an effective public speaker, attacking the 'November criminals' who had set up the republic. He urged an end to German subservience to foreign powers and demanded a dictatorship – with he himself evidently the dictator.[6] His outlook was strikingly antisemitic. The one and only way to break with the international moneylenders was 'to solve the Jewish question'.[7] After France occupied the Ruhr early in 1923, his target was not the French but the German government, calling for a settling of accounts with perfidious Jews and Social Democrats which must be carried out without sentimentality and with a 'merciless fury'.[8] The French prime minister, Raymond Poincaré, expressed alarm about extremist groups propagating the 'legend' that Germany had not been defeated in the war but had been paralysed by revolution, a 'legend' which, he added, was being used to discredit successive administrations and disrupt the payment of reparations.

Hitler's failed putsch in association with Ludendorff later that same year led to his imprisonment, removing him at the moment when economic recovery helped to strengthen parliamentary politics. It did not stop discussion of the war's end from continuing to be highly toxic. One member of an official inquiry argued, controversially, that the upheaval of 1918 was caused by military setbacks stemming from the failure of Ludendorff's over-ambitious spring offensive. Publication of the committee of inquiry's report was vetoed by the cabinet. At the same time the Head of State, Friedrich Ebert, hounded by journalists about his past, sued for libel in the courts, only to be convicted of having acted treasonably through his wartime involvement with a strike committee in the munitions industry. This effectively ruled him out of running for a second term and hastened his premature death.[9] His successor as President was the elderly Hindenburg, champion of the 'stab in the back' claim.

In the referendum in late 1929 on the American-sponsored Young Plan, which scheduled a scaling down of Germany's reparations, the National Socialists openly accused 'all-Jewish high finance' of being behind Germany's economic enslavement. Although the campaign was lost, the publicity was nevertheless timely. When the impact of the Wall Street Crash began to be fully felt, German unemployment climbed rapidly. Support for the party, by now committed to the constitutional overthrow of the republic, doubled in the 1930 election. Hitler, adept at fusing his personal struggle with his country's struggle for liberation, reaped the rewards from identifying democracy with capitulation and chaos. While his chances of office were remote, an English journalist judged, it was 'quite astonishing what fears and apprehensions this man creates'.[10] His call for a special tribunal to prosecute those who had brought disaster upon the Fatherland was a case in point, though he did seem to tone down his antisemitism. Support doubled yet again in the election of July 1932, and although the party's share of the vote fell back in the subsequent election that November, the Nazis were already established as the largest party in the Reichstag.

Invited to lead a right-wing coalition government, Hitler soon converted his temporary appointment as Chancellor into a position of permanence, aided by the passage of emergency legislation. Fundamental rights were suspended and opponents imprisoned without judicial redress. State policy was geared to 'the needs of the German people'. His coming to power, Hitler made plain, was only the prelude to rebuilding Germany, repudiating the Treaty of Versailles and re-instilling a martial spirit, materially and psychologically. He talked peace but was quite prepared to risk using bluff, bullying and even the threat of the use of arms in pursuit of expansionist aims, adjusting to changing circumstances and different audiences. His overriding preoccupation was to avoid the 'errors' of the Kaiser's reign.

His starting-point was the conviction that a united Germany was an invincible Germany. Conflict, in the modern setting, meant a contest between rival social systems. The victorious nation was the one with the greater social solidarity, unaffected by internal strife and capable of unquestioning sacrifice. Put to the test, a truly German state would never succumb in the way it had in 1918. According to some reports, Hitler was strengthened in this belief by a conversation with David Lloyd George (Britain's wartime prime minister) in 1936. Lloyd George, 'intentionally or inadvertently', left him with the impression that England had been about to fall apart and that Germany had given in too soon. Hitler had agreed, telling Lloyd George that the tragedy for Germany was that it had surrendered at 'five minutes to twelve' – 'if ever there is another war between Germany and England, Germany will fight on until twelve minutes [sic] after twelve o'clock, so long as I am *Führer*'.[11]

Unity required the creation of a single, disciplined, racially untainted national community, purged of 'unreliable' elements. Germany's half-a-million Jews were gradually stripped of influence, driven from public and social life, expelled from the professions and silenced in the press. The Nuremberg Laws (1935) deprived them of German citizenship. Once rearmament was under way, the economy was 'Aryanised' by taking over all Jewish-owned businesses. The resulting exodus, brought about by a variety of coercive means, diminished but did not entirely eliminate 'the Jewish peril' in Germany's midst. The appalling attacks on *Kristallnacht*[12], which occurred soon after the signing by Britain and France, in Munich, of a deal obliging Czechoslovakia to cede its German-speaking areas to Germany, caused a further significant surge in emigrants, expedited by threats in *Das Schwarze Korps* (the SS newspaper) that the Jews of Germany would be ghettoised and in due course wiped out by 'fire and sword'.[13] In 'internationalising' the issue, as Hitler told Goering, he could offer to send the richer Jews off 'to North America, Canada or some other large territory', exporting antisemitism into the bargain.[14]

Should it come to pass, a future war would, crucially, be a propaganda war. Hitler had a wary respect for the work of the British, French and American press which, having already invented stories of Prussian atrocities in 1914, did so much to blunt the impact of Ludendorff's last great offensive by highlighting the general strike in Germany, reviving Allied optimism. This, coming so soon after President's Wilson's Fourteen-Point peace proposal, had a devastating effect, fatally damaging public backing in Germany for the war effort. By spreading the 'poison' that Germany's cause was hopeless, the Allies softened up the other Central Powers, encouraging them to drop out. So too the issuing of the Balfour Declaration (supporting a Jewish homeland in Palestine) which wore down pro-German feeling in eastern Europe. It followed that great care should be taken to guard against anyone, especially Jewish schemers, trying to drive a wedge between the German people and its leaders.

Since Germany was surrounded by hostile states intent on preventing it from recovering its pre-eminence, all actions – including military ones – were justifiable actions in self-defence which Germany was 'forced' into by warmongers, both capitalist and communist. Strategy had to take full account of this reality. There could be no repetition of a two-front war in both eastern and western Europe. Difficulties should be tackled one-by-one. The long, costly slog of trench warfare was unsustainable. What was needed were short military campaigns and quick conquests, so that morale was maintained, casualties minimised and excessive strain was not put on the domestic economy.[15] Vital land must be acquired to make Germany self-sufficient, overcoming the effects of another economic blockade. Germany could become a great continental power, but only if the two extra-European world powers – the United States and the Soviet Union – were discouraged from intervening.

Germany, Hitler protested, had been taught a bitter lesson. By taking every possible precaution, the National Socialist state was ready 'for all eventualities'.

Notes

1.   L. Fraser, *Germany Between Two Wars: A Study of Propaganda and War Guilt* (London: Oxford University Press, 1944), p.16. The British officer in question denied using this turn of phrase. Hindenburg told a parliamentary inquiry in November 1919 that he still stood by all the decisions taken by the High Command and that the core of the army was sound. Operations miscarried because of 'clandestine disruption' causing weakness and indiscipline in the hinterland in the closing stages of the war (*Erklärung des Generalfeldmarschalls von Hindenburg vor dem Parlamentarischen Untersuchungsausschuß* ['Dolchstoßlegende'], 18 November 1919). Accessed on 3 February 2021 from: http://www.1000dokumente.de/index.html?c=dokument_de&dokument=0026_dol&object=pdf&st=&l=de.

2.   C. Falls, *Was Germany Defeated in 1918?* (Oxford: Clarendon Press, 1940). The German revolution of 1918-19, the author argued, was 'the consequence, not the cause, of defeat' (p.6). See also D. Welch's *Germany and Propaganda in World War 1 – Pacifism, Mobilization and Total War* (London: I.B. Tauris, 2014).

3.   See the summary of an article in the *Bayerischer Kurier* of 6 December 1918, in *Le Bulletin Périodique de la Presse Allemande* (No.101), covering 3-10 December 1918.

4.   Quoted in *Le Bulletin Périodique de la Presse Allemande* (No.96), covering 13-22 October 1918.

5.   *Die Salzburger Wacht*, reporting on one early meeting (in its issue of 6 October 1920), talked of a long-winded speech by Hitler which was greeted with resounding laughter.

6.   *Die Kreuzzeitung*, 28 December 1922.
8.   *Das Vorarlberger Tagblatt*, 10 July 1920.
9.   *Der Berliner Börsen-Courier*, 7 February 1923.
10. The first Chancellor of the republic, Ebert, had publicly greeted returning soldiers by calling them members of an 'unvanquished' army.
11. *The Manchester Guardian*, 26 September 1930.
12. 'Hitler may have been misled by Lloyd George, valet says', in *The St Petersburg Times* (Florida), 3 November 1955. See also the comments attributed to Hermann Goering in D.C. Poole, 'Light on Nazi Foreign Policy', in *Foreign Affairs*, 25, 1 (October 1946), p.132.
13. During the night of 9-10 November 1938, synagogues across Germany were set alight and Jewish-owned shops demolished by gangs of Nazi Party members.
14. Reported in *The Milwaukee Journal*, 23 November 1938.
15. Nuremberg document 1816-PS, recording remarks made by Goering during a conference on the elimination of Jews from the German economy, 10 November 1938, in *Trial of the Major War Criminals before the International Military Tribunal*, XXVIII (Nuremberg: 1948), pp.538-9. Goering, in the course of this meeting, openly stated that if war came there would be a showdown with Jewry.
16. The British Military Attaché in Berlin, in January 1937, was already pointing to the possibility of Hitler embarking upon 'short wars with limited objectives' (Quoted in F. Hinsley et al, *British Intelligence in the Second World War – its Influence on Strategy and Operations*, 1((London: HMSO, 1979)), p.76).

2

The Speech

Hitler's set-piece address to the opening session of the new Greater German Reichstag in January 1939 is, in this regard, a key exhibit. It was, in his usual style, a rambling statement, interspersed with the occasional bold declaration with which he, as one French newspaper put it, 'tells the world', the German people and even his own immediate entourage, 'of the decisions of the Reich'.[1] Largely moderate in tone, diplomats drew the reassuring conclusion that after the drama of the Munich agreement no new foreign policy initiatives were impending. But in one passage Hitler turned to 'the Jewish question'. Germany and indeed the whole of Europe, he asserted, would never live in peace until this issue was faced up to. Referring sarcastically to the failure of other countries to accept a greater number of Jewish emigrants, he insisted there was plenty of room for the Jews to be resettled elsewhere, so long as they understood the need for productive employment. Otherwise they would sooner or later become the victims of 'a crisis of unimaginable proportions'. He then delivered what he called a 'prophecy'. Jewish spokesmen, abusing the freedom of the press to unsettle world opinion, were attempting to stir up conflict and profit from the bloodshed. Germany and Italy, because they had broken the grip of 'rootless' propagandists, were the only two nations in a position to expose the danger of another pointless bloodbath. If, he warned menacingly, wagging his finger and raising his voice, 'the Jews of international finance in and outside Europe should succeed once more in plunging people into a general war, then the outcome would not be the Bolshevisation of the world and with it a victory for Jewry but – on the contrary – the annihilation of the Jewish race in Europe!'[2]

What on earth did he mean? Many observers found the claim too outlandish to take seriously. It could signify everything or nothing. Was he really proposing to lead 'a global antisemitic crusade?'[3]

Hitler's speeches are rightly recognised as a valuable, if not unique, source of historical evidence. He wrote little, disliked tying his hands and preferred passing on many of his commands verbally. His public utterances were, at least, incontrovertibly his own words. They express what he believed, or wanted others to believe – and this is the difficulty. Looking back in the 1950s and 1960s, many took his 'prophecy' to have been an explicit threat in advance to annihilate the Jewish population of Europe. Given what transpired, it seemed all too obviously self-evident. Subsequent research paid more attention to the context of the address, stressing Hitler's desire to speed up Jewish emigration from Germany by arousing the international community while simultaneously seeking to deter the United States from 'interfering' again in European affairs.[4] Since then, viewpoints have swung back somewhat. Hitler did make the 'good behaviour' of Jews at home and abroad an important criterion, utilising the Jewish issue as leverage. But it was not purely and simply a diplomatic trick. One current interpretation is that, while he wanted to pressurise America into accepting Germany's territorial demands, his comments did embody an apocalyptic image of racial destruction should a wider war break out.[5]

In an associated move a few days before Hitler spoke, Hermann Goering, the Reich Plenipotentiary for the Four-Year Plan, had appointed Reinhard Heydrich, chief of the Security Police and the Secret State Police (the Gestapo), to take charge of a new Reich Central Office for Jewish Emigration, 'to be advanced by all means', increasing the volume of emigrants and determining where they should emigrate to.[6] The regime, so it appeared, felt strong enough to tackle the matter head on, irritated by the hypocrisy of the 'humanitarian' democracies. But it was also only too willing to make use of Germany's 200,000 remaining Jews – and indeed Europe's Jews altogether – as valuable hostages, which would make their co-religionists abroad think twice about antagonising the new Germany. Goebbels, who facilitated the 'spontaneous' attacks on Jewish property in November, certainly did not hold back. Everyone could see that an 'anonymous force', prominent in the US, was seeking to whip up a war psychosis. This force, of course, was 'the Jews'. Furthermore, he wrote:

> If, one day, a new world war should unfortunately break out, the cry 'it's all the fault of the Jews!'…must echo across our continent. They are the ones who want war and who are doing everything in their power to push the people into a war. They themselves think they won't be the victims but the profiteers of such a war. This was why, across the whole world, they were behind the satanic campaign of excitation against Germany and Italy, and were calling for a military grouping by the democracies…[7]

In January 1939, an open war still seemed to be avoidable. By August, after Hitler had swallowed up the other parts of Czechoslovakia, it was more or less inevitable. The shock signing of the Nazi-Soviet Non-Aggression Pact led in short order to the German invasion of Poland and a division of the spoils with the Soviet Union, the pretext being that the Poles, egged on by Anglo-French plotting, were waiting for the right moment to attack Germany. Eradicating the Polish elites, Hitler was free to reorganise Polish territory according to German dictates. This included, as he mentioned in October, 'an attempt at settling the Jewish problem', apparently as part of a wider programme of population transfers of various ethnic minorities.[8] Nazi spokesmen 'had always stated that one of the results of the war would be the extermination of the 6 million Israelites of Central and Eastern Europe', the author of one survey of post-invasion Poland wrote. 'The actions of the conqueror, without confirming this forecast, have not disproved it.'[9] Details of a project for a Jewish enclave near Nisko in a remote part of the region of Lublin, when they materialised, suggested that some 60,000 Jews were to be uprooted from other parts of Poland as well as from Austria and the former Czechoslovakia and even from the Reich itself, and concentrated in an extended labour camp guarded by SS detachments under the command of a certain Eichmann. Eichmann (born in 1906 in the Rhineland but raised in Austria) was said to have played an active part on *Kristallnacht* by sacking a synagogue[10] and had masterminded the emigration in 1938 and 1939 of a large proportion of the Jewish population of Vienna.[11] The first arrivals, abandoned in bleak, inhuman conditions, with access only to contaminated wells, were soon perishing from hunger and cold.[12]

Now that the troops were at the front, Hitler called on all Germans to do their duty. The British doubted that Nazi Germany was as internally united as Imperial Germany had been, and said they could take advantage of this vulnerability. But 'pious preaching' by Britain and France would not work, in Hitler's view, because his nation was fully prepared. Dropping 'idiotic' leaflets by air to try to trigger 'another 1918' underestimated the willpower not just of the German army but of the German people. Germany was not going to make the same mistake twice. World Judaism was lined up against Germany. They had got the war they had been agitating for. As such, all Jews and non-Aryans were serving the cause of the adversary, making each and every one of them an enemy of the state.

The swift defeat of France in May and June 1940, and the withdrawal of British troops back across the English Channel, achieved in six weeks what Germany had been unable to do in the entire four years of the Great

War. It also opened up a new possibility for consolidating Germany's growing empire by excluding all opponents, actual and potential. The Jews, according to the German press, had made Europe 'a blood-soaked battlefield'. They, the 'scum of humanity', must suffer the consequences. A condition of the peace treaty in the west must be their banishment from European soil.[13] 'Physically annihilating' a people was rejected as 'fundamentally un-Germanic' by Himmler[14], and Hitler agreed given that Britain would have to give way to German force of arms. This did not bar him from taunting 'provocateurs' – Jewish émigrés in London and New York – who were playing 'the trumpets of Jericho'. Alfred Rosenberg, the ideologist of the Nazi Party, publicly promoted a Europe-wide plan to forcibly eject Jewry from the continent, shipping them off to a 'heavily policed' area overseas, such as the French island of Madagascar. The Nisko scheme, which had been obstructed by the Governor-General in occupied Poland, Hans Frank, who disliked 'wild' resettlements, was scrapped by Goering, and Eichmann's office – with representatives in place in Prague, Bratislava and Paris – was put to work fleshing out Rosenberg's proposal. Providing Britain saw sense and gave up its futile opposition, Rosenberg assumed, a real peace would be conceivable.

Hitler had not forgotten his Reichstag speech.[15] Vexed by Anglo-American intransigence, the 'pro-war' Jewish lobby in New York having 'rigged' Roosevelt's re-election in November 1940, he revived his threats in the new year. Should the 'other world' be plunged into a general war by Jewry, as he had 'already once said'[16], then Jewry, the 'inner foe', will have exhausted its role in Europe. Some might laugh at his prediction, as they had laughed in the past, he remarked. But he was certain he would be shown to have been right, as 'the coming months and years would demonstrate' – an avowal which, on this occasion, was widely viewed as a cautionary word to America not to take Britain's side. They were not dealing, he explained, with a worn out Germany (as President Wilson had been) but a Germany that had reconquered much of the territory it had lost and was mobilised to the highest degree, such that, in Goebbels's words, the whole country had taken a vow that November 1918 would never be repeated. Churchill's attempted appeals to the German public were 'a drunkard's ravings'. 'Leading Jewish intimates' of the President, the German embassy in Washington reported, were pressing Congress to approve the delivery of war material to the UK.[17] With the announcement of American Lend–Lease aid to Britain in March 1941, Hitler, in his so-called 'Purim' speech,[18] pointed out that no help 'coming from any part of the world' could rescue the British Empire. He blamed 'international finance' and Jewish 'plutocracy' for sparking off the conflict. He then applied an extra twist of the knife. The end of the war – 'completed' by the end of the year – 'will and must be their destruction'. In reprisal for the US decision, Nazi newspapers spoke of 'a heavy burden of responsibility' resting on the shoulders of those Jews who had emigrated and those still living in Europe.[19]

A 'hate-filled' coalition had successfully conspired to wage war on Germany; it was Hitler's duty to bring that war to a victorious close. Britain's stubbornness, its 'stupidity and arrogance', was the pivotal factor. Intrigues in the Balkans, ascribed to the British Ambassador to Moscow Sir Stafford Cripps, preyed on Hitler's mind, eventually forcing him to reroute several Poland-bound armoured divisions in order to occupy Yugoslavia and Greece. Convinced that Britain was helpless, utterly reliant on American assistance and clinging on to the hope of Russia changing sides, he arrived at a momentous decision. Germany could not endure another ruinous war on two fronts. As things stood, there was no western front on the mainland of Europe. The Tripartite Pact of September 1940, in which Germany, Italy and Japan undertook to assist each other, 'had the goal of frightening America'[20], supplemented by regular reminders that US meddling in European affairs 'would lead to intensified persecution of Jews in Germany and other Nazi-occupied countries'.[21] Hitler felt he must act while there was time. He now resolved to switch the might of his army onto his eastern ally, the Soviet Union, staking everything on a rapid toppling of Soviet power. Once Russia was out of the war, Britain would have no other option but to give up the fight. In the meantime, Germany would take control of the vital minerals and grain of Ukraine and southern Russia. The doubts of his generals were overridden, the machinations of 'Ambassador Cripps' (who was accurately forecasting a German attack) yet further proof of the way the British were trying to induce the Russians into playing a 'double game'.[22]

Hitler's public proclamation was relayed by Goebbels. The Soviet Union had, for the previous twenty years, been the chief inciter of misery and famine across Europe, actively seeking 'to set not only Germany but the whole of Europe aflame' in a vivid expression of the Jewish will to dominate.[23] It had, though allied to Germany, breached the terms of their 1939 pact by invading the Baltic states and massing troops on the German frontier. With British and American connivance, egged on by those war-hungry Jewish militants he had repeatedly warned about, it wanted to tie down and defeat the German Reich, which was why he had decided to put the future of Germany 'in the hands of its soldiers'. Here, too, he had an old score to settle, linked to the founding mythology of Hitlerism. It had been the German government which had given Lenin safe passage back into Russia in 1917, resulting in the downfall of Tsarism but also, by the 'disastrous' exporting of revolutionary influences into Germany, the crumbling of the German war effort. His gamble was designed to rectify that historic blunder, eradicating 'Judeo-Bolshevism' once and for all.

Notes

1. *Le Temps*, 1 February 1939.
2. Newsreel accessed on 3 February 2021 from: https://collections.ushmm.org/search/catalog/irn1000273. The exclamation mark was used in all the original reports of the speech.
3. The unofficial American diplomatic reaction, as reported in *Le Journal des Débats Politiques et Littéraires*, 1 February 1939.
4. H. Mommsen, 'Hitler's Reichstag Speech of 30 January 1939', in *History and Memory*, 9, 1-2 (Fall 1997), pp.147-61.
5. P. Burrin, *Ressentiment et Apocalypse – Essai sur L'antisémitisme Nazi* (Paris: Seuil, 2004).
6. Nuremberg document NG-2586-A in *Trials of War Criminals before the Nuernberg Military Tribunals*, XIII (Washington, DC: US Government Printing Office, 1952), pp.129-30.
7. *Völkischer Beobachter*, 1 April 1939.
8. *Neuigkeits Welt-Blatt*, 7 October 1939.
9. *Paix et Droit*, Octobre-Decembre 1939.
10. C. Lanzmann, *Le Dernier des Injustes* (Paris: Gallimard, 2015), pp.42-4.
11. That Eichmann did not just organise this process but created the position, the task and the methods is emphasised by Barbara Stangneth in her *Eichmann before Jerusalem – The Unexamined Life of a Mass Murderer* (London: The Bodley Head, 2014).
12. *Paix et Droit*, Janvier-Mars 1940.
13. *The St Petersburg Times* (Florida), quoting *Das Schwarze Korps*, 8 August 1940.
14. Memorandum by Himmler, 'Reflections on the Treatment of Peoples of Alien Races in the East', of 25 May 1940, in *Trials of War Criminals before the Nuernberg Military Tribunals*, XIII (Washington, DC: US Government Printing Office, 1952), pp.147-50.
15. Mommsen thought so, suggesting Hitler was only reminded of it when Goebbels included a clip of the speech in his pseudo-documentary film, *Der Ewige Jude* (The Eternal Jew) in November 1940.
16. From this point on, as Max Domarus was one of the first to notice, Hitler misdated his January 1939 prophecy by placing it at the start of the war in September 1939. See M. Domarus, *Hitler: Speeches and Proclamations 1932-1945*, 1 (1990), p.41 (the English translation of a work originally published in German in 1963).
17. The German embassy in the US to the German Foreign Ministry, Document 88, 26 February 1941, in *Documents on German Foreign Policy 1918-1945*, D, XII (Washington, DC: US Government Printing Office, 1962), pp.161-2.
18. *The Chicago Sentinel*, 20 March 1941. Purim is a Jewish festival celebrating the saving in the biblical Book of Esther of the Jewish people from massacre.

19. *The Ohio Jewish Chronicle*, 21 March 1941.

20. See Ribbentrop's comments to the Japanese Ambassador on 27 March 1941, in R. Sontag and J.Beddie (eds), *Nazi-Soviet Relations 1939-1941* (Washington, DC: US Department of State, 1948), p.287.

21. *The Ohio Jewish Chronicle*, 6 June 1941. The newspaper said that after a strong anti-Nazi speech by Roosevelt the German press was demanding all Jews should be ousted from Berlin, 1,000 having already been evicted from their homes in various cities in order to give shelter to 'Aryans' made homeless by British bombing.

22. S. Burgess, *Stafford Cripps – A Political Life* (London: Gollancz, 1999), pp.141-2.

23. *Volks Zeitung*, 23 June 1941.

3

Special Tasks

Operation Barbarossa – the codename for the surprise German invasion of the Soviet Union on 22 June 1941 – began spectacularly. Just before dawn three million German and other Axis troops poured across the entire length of Russia's European border, catching the Soviet army completely unawares. In the following days entire Soviet divisions were outflanked and encircled, with huge losses of men and equipment. By the third week of the offensive, the Dniepr river had been reached, Leningrad was in danger and German tank columns were approaching the city of Smolensk, the gateway to Moscow. German military commanders were hopeful that the war in the east was, to all intents and purposes, already won.

On 16 July, with every prospect of soon finishing off the Red Army as a fighting force, Hitler met with a small group of his closest collaborators – Goering, Alfred Rosenberg (Hitler's choice as Minister-in-waiting for the Occupied Eastern Territories), Field Marshal Keitel, his Chief of Staff, and Hans-Heinrich Lammers, head of the Reich Chancellery – at his advance headquarters at Rastenburg in East Prussia. The meeting started at 3pm and lasted until just before 8pm. A note of what was said was kept by Martin Bormann, Hitler's new private secretary. It is mainly from his pencilled draft that we have a sense of Hitler's grandiose ambitions.[1] His colleagues were expecting to discuss how they were going to administer the steadily enlarging zone in the Baltic, eastern Poland and western Ukraine that German soldiers were now in possession of, ironing out by 'the will of the *Führer*' the jurisdictional disagreements that had been left hanging over from the preparatory phase of the campaign. In the event, annoyed by an 'impudent' article in a Vichy French newspaper claiming that the war against the Soviet Union was a war being waged by Europe and that Europe as a whole should reap the benefit, Hitler presented his guests at the outset with 'some fundamental statements' involving matters that had to be considered 'without delay'.

His most pressing concern was to nail down the preconditions for German mastery. They should explain to the inhabitants of areas which had fallen under their control that Germany had, of course, been acting in self-protection – his notion of a preventative war – and by occupying territory they would bring order and provide for the means of existence. Tactically, it suited them to pretend to be 'freeing' people from Bolshevism. In practice, he went on, though they should not say so publicly, much of the east must be incorporated into the Greater German Reich. Germany's presence was final and for good, and they had no intention of ever leaving. To enforce this on the ground, there was nothing to stop 'our taking all necessary measures – shooting, resettling etc. – and we shall take them'. The chief objective was to control, organise and exploit, pacifying the vast region through the German monopoly of arms. Since Stalin had recently issued a call for partisan warfare, this gave Germany the broadest possible excuse, Hitler urged, 'to eradicate everyone who opposes us'. Under no circumstances should occupation policy, as it had in Alsace in 1914-18, be 'wavering'. They had to do what the British had always done in India, single-mindedly pursuing one line and one aim, subduing opposition with complete pitilessness. Rosenberg's preference (he mentions it in his diary[2]) for trying try to win over the eastern peoples was quickly dismissed, Goering interjecting that the priority was to strip Ukraine of its abundant food supplies. The best solution was 'to shoot anybody who looked askance'. Hitler's goal was a Germanised 'Garden of Eden' in the newly-won east, 'protected against all possible dangers', and with the Slavs pushed back beyond the Ural mountains. This was not (as the Vichy newspaper presented it) Germany fighting for the cause of Europe, but the imposition of long-lasting German rule.

The Jewish question was not openly referred to in so many words, so far as one can tell. Nonetheless the Soviet Union in Hitler's demonological world view was not only the embodiment of Jewish despotism. It was also the ancestral breeding ground of Jewry. To defeat such an opponent necessitated an entirely unprecedented, far more brutal kind of battle in which the usual international norms would not apply. He had spelled this out beforehand to the heads of the German armed services, instructing them about the nature of the combat they were about to encounter. The coming conflict would be 'a war of extermination' based on racial difference. If Germany was to win, it would have to act with 'unmerciful and unrelenting harshness'. All Soviet Commissars (Communist Party officials attached to the military) were to be 'liquidated', along with the Jewish-Bolshevist intelligentsia. Any breaking of international law by German soldiers would be overlooked. The Soviet Union was not a signatory to the Hague Convention on Land Warfare and, as such, had no rights.[3] It was essential to think in terms of generations to come. Unless

Germany acted firmly while they had the chance, they would be faced in 30 years' time with a resurgent Communist adversary.

Two top secret directives were subsequently issued on Hitler's orders. In the first, the infamous 'Commissar Order', political commissars – 'the true pillars of resistance' – were to be treated 'promptly' and, if captured in fighting or resisting capture, were to be shot immediately.[4] The second stipulated that all offences committed by enemy non-combatants should be dealt with not by courts-martial but by the officer on the spot, who would decide whether they were to be executed.

In addition to these army-specific guidelines, Heinrich Himmler had been assigned a series of 'special tasks' – again on Hitler's direct orders – relating to the administration of areas where the army was operating and for which he was solely and personally responsible. Among these tasks was the deployment of specially-constituted police units, supervised by Heydrich, now heading an enlarged Reich Main Security Office (*Reichssicherheitshauptamt* or RSHA) and charged with identifying and combating subversive activities. Four *Einsatzgruppen,* totalling some 3,000 SS, Gestapo and police officers, were to single out and eliminate key individuals, among them officials of the Communist Party, radical elements and Jews occupying posts in the party and government. They were also meant to whip up anti-Jewish pogroms by the local population. As Keitel himself later admitted, while supposedly protecting the army in the rear the special units were to undertake a policy of racial cleansing.

In the wake of the German advance, these rules of engagement were liberally construed. The German press told its readers that the 'Jewish military and political leadership' of the Soviet Union knew it was in a life-or-death struggle of competing world views 'to the last drops of blood'.[5] The 'scorched earth' approach adopted by the retreating Soviet army was soon being pinned on the Jew, the '*weltbrandstifter*', the universal arsonist. As some of the crimes committed by the NKVD, the Soviet secret police, became known about, the first hints emerged of German contingents carrying out 'retaliatory' attacks on Jews wherever they were encountered.

At this point, there was no generalised diktat to murder Jewish civilians as a whole. The defence put forward by members of the *Einsatzgruppen* at their post-war trial, maintaining that they were given an all-encompassing order prior to the start of Barbarossa, is no longer credible.[6] Jews, especially adult male Jews, were just one category among several targets. But as Hitler was making perfectly plain and emphasising to other senior army officers, they should spread 'such terror as is likely, by its mere existence, to crush every will to resist'[7], and in this respect the Jews were foremost. Hitler's 'fundamental statements' to do with partisans, saboteurs and other obstructive groups were an incitement to escalate the killing of ungovernable 'subhumans'.

When, therefore, the conference at Hitler's headquarters eventually discussed the dividing up of competencies, Hitler was unshakeable. Rosenberg, having lost the economic power of decision to Goering, had been grumbling about the excessive authority of Himmler, whose 'special tasks' threatened to amount to a parallel government in the east which would not be subordinate to his own ministry. For some weeks Bormann had been siding with Himmler. The moment had come for Hitler's 'clarification'. Although Himmler's bid for a 'political' policing role was refused, it would be incorrect to assume his wings were clipped.[8] As the minutes show, 'the *Führer*, the Reich Minister [Goering] and others reiterate that Himmler was to have no greater jurisdiction than he had in Germany proper, but this [much] was absolutely necessary', Hitler seeking to mollify Rosenberg with the comment that their quarrel would soon subside. In this way, despite his curious absence from the meeting, the Jewish issue remained Himmler's no-go preserve.[9] On the following day, after lunching with Heydrich and Lammers and finalising the decree confirming his brief for securing the eastern areas, Himmler authorised a five-fold increase in the number of auxiliary police units which were to work in conjunction with the *Einsatzgruppen*. Hitler also, it should be noted, stated that non-observance of the Hague Convention was to carry over into the civil administration of the former Soviet Union, on the basis that the Soviet Union was ceasing to exist.[10]

One further indication of intent was apparent from an agreement at this point between Hitler and Goebbels to give greater emphasis to the 'Jewish character' of the war.[11] The Propaganda Ministry had not had the opportunity to prepare the German public for the sudden attack on Russia, and many Germans were still perplexed by the new course. An inspired editorial in the *Deutsche Allgemeine Zeitung*, the mouthpiece of the German Foreign Office, argued that events were moving in the anticipated direction.[12] The coming together of the war in the east and the news of Anglo-American offers to help the Russians were all part of the world Jewish plot against Germany, an anti-Nazi coalition of 'Bolshevism' and 'Plutocracy', in just the way Hitler had foreseen in his prophetic speech of January 1939 – a speech which the Jews, being so 'brainy', 'may have heard of'. Because it was a Jewish-instigated war, what Hitler had expected was taking place. Roosevelt, the American President in hock to Wall Street, was trying to re-establish a Jewish stranglehold on the European continent. His 'provocation policy' was, perversely, only aggravating 'the Jewish question'. Germany and its allies – France was mentioned – were taking the appropriate steps together. All Roosevelt's efforts, as Goebbels and others crowed, were doomed. Given the rapidity of the German onslaught, the US would not be able to react in time to save the Soviet Union, a slave state built by Jews and ruled by Jews, from defeat. Hitler's many warnings had not been heeded. The end result, 'sooner or later', would be a resource-rich, impregnable Europe under German leadership, unified and 'Jew-free'.

Notes

1.   *Nazi Conspiracy and Aggression*, VII (Washington, DC: US Government Printing Office, 1946), pp.1086-1093. Accessed on 5 February 2021 from: https://www.loc.gov/rr/frd/Military_Law/NT_Nazi-conspiracy.html.

2.   J. Matthäus and F. Bajohr (eds), *The Political Diary of Alfred Rosenberg* (Lanham, MD: Rowman & Littlefield, 2015), entry dated 20 July 1941.

3.   The convention outlawed the ill-treatment of Prisoners of War and civilians, as well as looting and other forms of wilful destruction.

4.   'Directives for the Treatment of Political Commissars', 6 June 1941. Accessed on 5 February 2021 from: http://germanhistorydocs.ghi-dc.org/sub_document.cfm?document_id=1548.

5.   *Der Südostdeutsche Zeitung*, 4 July 1941.

6.   See especially the work of Alfred Streim – for example his 'The Tasks of the SS Einsatzgruppen' in *The Simon Wiesenthal Center Annual*, 4 (White Plains New York: Kraus International Publications, 1987). Accessed on 5 February 2021 from: https://www.museumoftolerance.com/education/archives-and-reference-library/online-resources/simon-wisenthal-center-annual-volume-4/annual-4-chapter-9.html.

7.   The expression used in the German High Command order of 22 July 1941, after Walther von Brauchitsch, Commander-in-Chief of the army, had consulted Hitler.

8.   'Political' policing related to Himmler's additional role of 'strengthening the German nation'.

9.   Otto Bräutigam, Rosenberg's liaison officer at HQ, confirmed that Himmler was present that morning at Rastenburg but otherwise occupied.

10. Rosenberg's diary is, admittedly, muddled on this point.

11. E. Fröhlich (ed.), *Die Tagebücher von Joseph Goebbels*, II, 1 (Munich: K.G. Saur, 1996), entry dated 9 July 1941.

12. *Deutsche Allgemeine Zeitung*, 13 July 1941.

4

The Commission

Europe was to become 'Jewless', but what exactly was in store for the many Jewish communities scattered across Europe? The few documents which survive, since they are contradictory and inconclusive, fail to supply a clear answer. Does this support the suggestion by some historians that the Nazi leadership, and above all Hitler, had not yet come to any definite decision?

In Hitler's inner circle, and amongst those officials and agencies with a vested interest, the project to 'evacuate' German and other European Jews was at a standstill. Jewish emigration from the continent had, in wartime conditions, greatly diminished, and in some cases was actively vetoed. The idea of relocating some or all of Europe's Jews to the French island of Madagascar, under examination since the fall of France, was out of the question so long as the British Royal Navy still controlled the seaways. Operation Barbarossa, by contrast, offered up the endless land tracts of the east, where a transplanted population could be dumped *en masse* and slowly worked or starved to death in the inhospitable climate. Policy adjusted to the prospects. The main outlines of an initial draft deportation scheme had been presented by Heydrich to Hitler in the spring of 1941 in line with his existing mandate from Goering. No copy of this scheme has ever been unearthed, but it is thought to have involved moving the roughly 5.8 million Jews of central and western Europe into the *General Gouvernement*, the German-occupied part of old Poland, seen as a convenient staging post before sending them further eastwards to 'a territory yet to be determined'. The scheme was, however, turned down by Hitler because of objections from the military in the build-up to the attack on Russia. He also halted the *ad hoc* deporting of Viennese Jews to the district of Lublin (again) after several thousand more had been shipped there. Hitler's inclination, often expressed in vitriolic terms[1], was to postpone matters until the war was over. The Jews of Germany and the rest of Europe were to 'disappear'. In spite of regular public references - Rosenberg talked of removing every single Jew from Europe 'even if it takes five, ten or twenty years'[2] - there was no cut-and-dried conception of how this would be done.

On the last day of July, two weeks after the Rastenburg conference, Goering received Heydrich at his ministry in Berlin. Complementing and extending the assignment he had given him in January 1939, Goering signed a brief, three-paragraph note commissioning Heydrich to make all necessary preparations and draw up a plan of action for 'the Final Solution [*die Endlösung*] of the Jewish Question' by 'emigration and evacuation' (evacuation being the new provision) in the whole of the German sphere of influence in Europe. All organisational, practical and financial aspects were to be taken into account in order to bring about the most favourable solution in the prevailing conditions.[3] In drawing up the plan, the other relevant governmental authorities were to be 'involved'. Two separate sources demonstrate that this fresh commission had the approval of Hitler.[4]

Of all the Holocaust records, Goering's *ermächtigung* is one of the most mystifying and disputed. Its format is odd, its meaning elusive, its purpose uncertain. Although it bears Goering's imprimatur, there is no printed letterhead and it was evidently typed up in the RSHA. The wording is bureaucratic, and the key expression –'final solution' – is opaque and, it would appear, intentionally so. Quite why it was composed and why at that stage remains a mystery.

The experts do not agree. At one time it was generally thought to be a, if not the, written Hitler 'order' to physically destroy the Jews, with Goering the go-between for setting in motion the whole murderous policy. Many now think of it as a much more mundane tool for asserting the RSHA's primacy in interdepartmental discussions. For some it still represents, in disguised form, a death warrant. Others prefer to think of it as just one marker in an unfolding process, only deserving of mention in a paragraph or two.[5] Götz Aly, drawing on the archives opened up in Moscow in the 1990s, has Heydrich noting in March 1941 that he had submitted a proposal about the Jewish question to Goering, 'which he approved after making a change with respect to Rosenberg's responsibilities and ordered its resubmission'. Aly assumes this was an earlier version of the *ermächtigung*.[6] Otherwise the existing evidence has been squeezed dry.

The heart of the puzzle is occupied by the man who may have drafted the *ermächtigung*, Adolf Eichmann, the head of the Gestapo's *judenreferat* or Jewish section. Having worked on the Nisko plan and the Madagascar project, Eichmann was, in all probability, also the author of Heydrich's aforementioned deportation scheme. A recent redesignation of departmental roles had given him a broader remit, from deportation *per se* to overall Jewish affairs, paving the way for monitoring and treating

Europe's Jewish population in a uniform fashion.[7] Eichmann's movements are critical to an understanding of what was brewing. In hiding as well as after his eventual capture in 1960, he spoke and wrote at length on many occasions. As his trial and his various confessions illustrate, however, he was a wholly unreliable narrator, slippery and evasive regarding his own doings. Responding to the claim he had prepared the *ermächtigung* and effectively written his own terms of reference, his denial – 'I had nothing whatsoever to do with this plan' – was unconvincing.[8] Can the abundance of online historical content now help to establish what he was up to?

Foreign press reports, particularly by correspondents from neutral countries in Berlin, are strangely underused. Reporting was subject to censorship and manipulation, but foreign journalists were often exceptionally well-informed. In some instances, their articles offer clues which an official document, by itself, cannot ever divulge.[9]

Two reports are especially interesting.

The first, from the New York-based Jewish Press Service, dates from the middle of July 1941 and relies on informants in the Baltic. It asserted that 'Herr Eichmann', the 'notorious' Gestapo officer responsible for Jewish affairs, had lately arrived in Lithuania on the heels of the German takeover. He had been sent there to suppress 'Jewish anti-Nazi activities' with the express aim of 'liquidating' the Lithuanian Jewish community. His appearance in Kaunas and Vilno, both towns with a large Jewish population, was creating panic. The JPS recalled the allegedly Palestinian-born, Hebrew-speaking Eichmann's part in the arrest and eviction of many thousands of Jews in pre-war Austria.[10]

There is much to notice. Eichmann is identified by name. The story has him turning up in Lithuania at the very time when shootings of local Jewish males had been going on for some days (above all in Vilno) and the German authorities were encouraging Jewish leaders to gather their community in dedicated 'living quarters', pretending it was for their own good. It also throws serious doubt on Eichmann's testimony that once the *Ostfeldzug* had begun he was desk-bound and his office was effectively sidelined. *Hamashkif*, a Tel Aviv daily, related that Eichmann's actions had been praised as 'exemplary'.[11]

The second report comes from the Swedish newspaper *Social Demokraten*, whose representative, Eric Lindqvist, had good contacts with the Swedish Legation in the German capital. It was dated 4 August. Writing about the highly sensitive issue of growing public antipathy to the war and of a clampdown on dissident circles, Lindqvist revealed that:

A senior SS leader, Eichmann, has been invested with full powers [*fullmakter*] for handling the German Jews, which in practice makes him a special dictator over them. He now has complete authority in this respect throughout Greater Germany and the occupied territories.[12]

His promotion, 'it is said', Lindqvist went on, 'has been found necessary to centralise the surveillance of the Jews' in the hands of an 'experienced' person. Thousands of wounded German soldiers were returning by train from the front. Air raids were also becoming more frequent. Germany's Jews were being picked on as the malcontents behind an underground 'opposition'. There were house searches to see if Jewish families were infringing various rules and regulations. Increased police activity was justified by the argument that the Jews and their international helpers had caused the war. In a follow-up despatch, Eichmann was said to have been given extra powers 'today', apparently entitling him 'to deal with the Jews in the Ukraine as seen fit', where, alongside his measures, the slaughtering of Jews was anticipated.[13]

It was quite a scoop on a number of counts. There is a clear if unstated knowledge of Goering's letter signed a day or two previously, granting powers amounting to a *vollmacht* or bestowal of absolute discretion. There is the equally important revelation that these sweeping powers, though Goering (we know) addressed himself to Heydrich, had been delegated to his Jewish expert, Eichmann, installing him in a 'dictatorial' position. To cap it all, Eichmann was to have a free hand not only in regard to the Jews of Germany but those too throughout Europe under German occupation, including in Rosenberg's Ukraine. It attributes to Eichmann a prominence in the making of Jewish policy that, much later on, even many of his accusers considered far-fetched.

For a journalist to have got wind of such a classified item of information in such a short space of time was a remarkable feat. One suspicion might be that it was purposely planted to enhance Eichmann's credentials. Goebbels is known to have used Swedish contacts in this way. Another witness refers to having read a story in the leading Danish newspaper, the *Berlingske Tidende*, that the Gestapo had created a special Jewish department headed by a high SS officer, Adolf Eichmann, no mention of which was made in the German press.[14]

These discoveries – leaks or not – shed new light on the meaning of Goering's commission.

Why was the document written when it was written? In many histories it seems to crop up out of the blue without explanation. In truth the *ermächtigung* was one of many initiatives flowing from the 16 July meeting, when the disagreements about Rosenberg's competence, which had been holding things up, were finally settled on the basis of Hitler's ruling in Himmler's favour. Rosenberg was plainly blocked off from Himmler's police and security duties in the occupied East, where the Jews were destined to shortly be moved. Heydrich went to and got Goering's full authority to draw up an 'evacuation' plan for effecting this.

How did the measures already being implemented on the eastern front relate – another poser – to the projected European solution? Eichmann's presence in some of the centres of Jewish settlement in the *Ostland,* as the Baltic states were now designated, was in order to oversee the registration and segregation of the Jewish population, serving, as Dina Porat's study of Lithuania demonstrates, as a test bed for techniques which were being tried out for the first time.[15] In the RSHA's guidelines standardising the handling of the Jewish question in regard to Soviet Jewry, drafted in late July or early August, however, officials had to bear in mind that the Jewish problem regarding the whole of Europe was to be solved by the end of the war 'at the latest' and that measures applied in the meantime were only 'preparatory' and 'partial' in view of the upcoming resettlement of Jews from the Reich.[16] The point was to break the Jewish hold over the Russian people by marking them and abolishing their freedom of movement by setting up ghettos and introducing forced labour. Given the 'brutality' of the fighting, the next step was to bring the struggle home, stigmatising Germany's own Jews by accusing them of violating wartime regulations, like the curfew, and harbouring Communist sympathies.

What, lastly, does it tell us about the state of thinking on the Jewish question? This is the biggest finding. Seventy-five per cent of all the Jews in the world were under Hitler's thumb, and a 'total world solution' was 'imminent'.[17] The object of the *ermächtigung* was to specify whose job it was to determine how the final goal – large-scale deportation – was to be achieved. It conferred upon Heydrich, and so upon Eichmann, the right to modify the existing draft plan to take account of the reality of a vast, expanding territory to the east, densely populated by Jews, and to draw up detailed arrangements which would then be submitted to his superiors. The commission left open exactly what form '*die Endlösung*' was to take. It also indicates that Eichmann had the ability not just to carry out policy but to fashion what that policy should be.[18] He did not occupy a minor role. He was one of the principal figures.

Notes

1. Hitler met Marshal Kvaternik, Commander-in-Chief of the Croatian armed forces, in late July, telling him that without Jews (this '*bazillusherd*') any longer in Europe, European unity would be assured; whether they were sent to Siberia or Madagascar was 'all the same' (*Akten zur Deutschen Auswärtigen Politik: 1918-1945*, D, XIII, 2 (Göttingen: Vandenhoeck & Ruprecht, 1970), p.838.

2. *Neues Wiener Tagblatt*, 29 March 1941.

3. Norbert Kampe suggests this wording was sufficiently flexible to allow for further development. See his 'Besprechung über der Judenfrage – Das Protokoll der Wannsee-Konferenz am 20 Januar 1942', in *Einsicht 07 – Bulletin des Fritz Bauer Instituts* (Spring 2012), p.18. Accessed on 8 February 2021 from: https://www.fritz-bauer-institut.de/fileadmi/editorial/publikationen/einsicht/einsicht-07.pdf.

4. See p.245 of the extracts from the memorandum by Martin Luther, Under Secretary of State in the German Foreign Office, of 21 August 1942, in *Trials of War Criminals before the Nuernberg Military Tribunals*, XIII (Washington, DC: US Government Printing Office, 1952); and the note by an *Ostministerium* official of 16 January 1942 quoted from by G. Aly and S. Heim in their *Vordenker der Vernichtung* (Hamburg: Hoffmann and Campe, 1991), p.469.

5. Compare Y. Bauer in 'Who was responsible and when? Some well-known documents revisited' in *Holocaust and Genocide Studies*, 6, 2 (June 1991), pp.129-149 with P. Longerich's *Holocaust – the Nazi Persecution and Murder of the Jews* (Oxford: Oxford University Press, 2010), pp. 260-1.

6. G. Aly, *Endlösung – Völkerverschiebung und der Mord an den Europäischen Juden* (Frankfurt a. M.: Fischer Verlag, 1998), p.270-1.

7. Aly, *ibid* (1998), pp.104-5, where he makes use of the RSHA organisational chart of 1 March 1941.

8. *The Trial of Adolf Eichmann*, 4 (Jerusalem: Trust for the Publication of the Proceedings of the Eichmann Trial: Israel State Archives, 1993). For an online version see the transcript of Session 92 of the trial. Accessed on 8 February 2021 from: http://www.nizkor.org/hweb/people/e/eichmann-adolf/transcripts/Sessions/Session-092-03.html.

9. Newspaper reports are not pure or unproblematic, and yet it is easy to forget they are a primary source, contemporary in time and usually provenanced, stemming from those whose business it is to find things out.

10. *The Chicago Sentinel*, 17 and 24 July 1941.

11. *Hamashkif*, 17 August 1941.

12. *Social Demokraten*, 3 August 1941; the Jewish Telegraphic Agency news bulletin, 5 August 1941. Accessed on 22 July 2021 from: HYPERLINK "redir.aspx?REF= KNffm4N4zWKGcWkINdov0EilKg7D0x9KYSEwdtaozdhuDrFMtU3ZCAFodHRwcz ovL3d3dy5qdGEub3JnLzE5NDEvMDgvMDUvYXJjaGl2ZS9nZXN0YXBvLXJlbmV3c ylhbnRpLWpld2lzaC10ZXJyb3ItaW4tdGhlLXJlaWNo"https://www.jta.org/1941/08/0 5/archive/gestapo-renews-anti-jewish-terror-in-the-reich.

13. Summarised in a report from Stockholm by the Jewish Telegraphic Agency news bulletin, 6 August 1941. The report is in part garbled.

14. See p.289 of E. Boehm's *We Survived* (New Haven, CT: Yale University Press, 1949).

15. D. Porat, 'The Holocaust in Lithuania – some unique aspects', in D. Cesarani (ed.), *The Final Solution – origins and implementation* (London and New York: Routledge, 1994), pp.159-74.

16. 'Richtlinien für die Behandlung der Judenfrage' (*Trial of the Major War Criminals before the International Military Tribunal*, XXV (Nuremberg: 1947), pp.302-6.

17. *Der Grenzbote* newspaper (Bratislava), quoted in *The Chicago Sentinel*, 4 September 1941.

18. All of which bears out the judgment of Y. Lozowick's *Hitler's Bureaucrats – The Nazi Security Police and the Banality of Evil* (London and New York: Continuum, 2002).

5

Paying the Price

Hitler's encouraging of his subordinates in mid-July to treat 'the Jewish enemy' with greater severity came at a point when German forces were still advancing and he was anxious to snuff out any signs of defiance from the Poles, Balts and Ukranians towards their new 'protectors'. By early August, the Soviet army had had time to regroup and German progress slowed on the approaches to Leningrad, Moscow and Kiev. German officers were forced to concede they had underestimated the tenacity of the Russian soldier. Guerrilla activity began to exacerbate the situation, characterised by the 'bestial' depravity of Russians ordered to stay behind by their Commissars and carry out Bolshevik 'banditry'.[1] Antisemitic propaganda was intensified. A booklet, *Germany Must Perish*, written by an obscure American businessman, Theodore Kaufman, was seized upon by Goebbels who, though he thought its contents 'absurd', publicized 'Roosevelt's plan' to sterilise the German people and carve up the Reich, employing it to show what to expect were Germany to be beaten for a second time in a generation.[2] Everything was done to present the war as an existential fight to destroy or be destroyed.

The transition from the selective killing of mainly adult Jewish males to a thorough, unqualified elimination of all Soviet Jews took place gradually in different locations in late July and early August. A directive to this effect was apparently issued by Himmler.[3] He also passed on instructions in person, visiting the leaders of the various *Einsatzgruppen*. Many thousands had so far been hunted down, executed and buried in quarries or freshly dug pits. Henceforth, women and children would not be spared, even if this meant SS and police units returning to areas they had already combed. *Deutschlandsender*, the German armed forces radio station in Belgrade whose transmitter was powerful enough to broadcast deep into Russia, released a *communiqué* in Russian on 2 August recalling that Germany had 'declared war on the Jews' at the outset of the struggle, deriding the feeble attempts by the English and the Soviets to join forces in the Far East and asserting that 'everything is moving towards the last settling of accounts, that is towards a massacre of the Jews without any exceptions'.[4]

Dieter Wisliceny, Eichmann's adviser in Slovakia, found out from Eichmann about what was being done and why. It was Wisliceny's understanding that Himmler and Heydrich simply stretched the covering authority of the 'Commissar Order' to include the entirety of Soviet Jewry that was falling under German control. The Jews *in toto* were 'hostile'. They were the nucleus of the stiffening resistance to German rule. Pockets of insurgents were more prevalent in Jewish-concentrated areas, posing a hazard to the army's supply lines. Jews, so long as they survived, could always attempt a future uprising. The threat had to be stamped out altogether.[5] Hitler was kept informed and regularly received confidential bulletins detailing the rising total of victims. In his night-time conversations in this period, he spoke disparagingly of the Jews, 'the inventors of Christianity' and the first to practice large-scale annihilation of whole peoples.[6]

Research by Wendy Lower on the evolution of occupation policy in Zhytomir in central Ukraine, using new documentation, backs up the notion of a radicalising trend.[7] In those areas in the Baltic states which were the first to be occupied, Jewish inhabitants, having been identified and put to work, were indeed moved to clearly demarcated ghetto settlements. Shooting was sporadic. In the western half of Ukraine, which was overrun in July but much less secure, Himmler's exhortations altered the way the Jews were treated. Mass murder meant that ghettos – outlined in the first instance in the RSHA guidance – were obsolete. Those arrested were temporarily confined in derelict buildings and small encampments before being shot. This pattern was not unvarying but was nevertheless pronounced. A case can be made that, even if the pre-Barbarossa instructions were to focus on Jews occupying important posts in the Soviet state, the ultimate intention all along was to widen the killing. Extending it by stages allowed the mobile units to become acclimatised to their grisly task. The German army learned to tolerate, even to participate, in the SS's actions. The prior elimination of adult males left the women and children without protection when the time came to eliminate them too. This case is negated, however, by Lower's study. There was a step-wise progression from partial to total obliteration, the impetus provided by Hitler and Himmler, that had not been originally contemplated.

On 9 and 10 August – while accounts of German units in Russia undertaking 'special tasks' started to filter through[8] – Churchill and Roosevelt met up (it was their very first meeting) in Placentia Bay, off

Newfoundland. They discussed how best to 'actively engage in resisting [Hitlerite] aggression', examining 'every corner of every continent'. Churchill was especially keen on fostering European democratic sentiment. They also talked about delivering war *matériel* to the Soviets. At the close they issued a joint declaration, the Atlantic Charter, promising 'the final destruction of the Nazi tyranny' and offering a guarantee to restore self-government to those who had been forcibly deprived of it. Churchill did not get what he hoped for, an American declaration of war on Germany. Even so, Roosevelt's approval of a set of common goals was a remarkably far-reaching commitment for a country that was, technically, neutral.

Hitler's immediate reaction is unclear. There are some sparse items of testimony. One report has it that he flew into a rage when he heard about the statement. His Foreign Minister, Joachim von Ribbentrop, later claimed they had a row while Hitler was unwell, Ribbentrop wondering aloud why Hitler was bent upon unnecessarily goading the Jewish lobby. The only unimpeachable source is the private journal of Goebbels.

In his capacity as propaganda supremo, Goebbels poured scorn on the Charter, comparing it to President Wilson's Fourteen Points and dismissing it as another piece of insolent Jewish-serving mischief, a gigantic bluff full of hollow, antiquated phrases. Germany could not be harmed because its people were not as gullible and its leaders were also cleverer. This time they knew what had to be done. A close watch was maintained on troublemakers. Senior figures in the Catholic Church, speaking out about the lawlessness of the Gestapo and the harassment of religious institutions, had for some time been a cause for concern. Clemens von Galen, the Bishop of Münster who had just been denouncing the practice of euthanasia, was regarded as particularly 'treacherous'. When Hitler, backtracking after public disapproval, suspended the T4 euthanasia programme in mid-August[9], several of his acolytes turned their anger on the Jews, who should be sorted out 'one way or another' (a favourite Hitler phrase) before the fighting in Russia had even concluded.

As Gauleiter of Berlin, Goebbels was also itching to ensure the capital would be the first wholly *judenfrei* German city. Complaints were being made by soldiers on leave, he asserted, who were astonished at the way Jews, subject to the 'severest' treatment in the east, were freely moving about town spreading misinformation. It was high time they wore some form of identifiable marking so that they could not pass themselves off as loyal citizens. 'Sweeping' action was needed and he would not 'let it go'.

Hitler's formula – no deportations until after the war – was still operative. It suited many state officials opposed to any rash changes.

Goebbels, sensing an opportunity, used the production of Goering's *ermächtigung*, obtained 'by some dark and forever secretive means'[10], to throw open the discussion.

The prime movers worked in unison. A full deportation scheme had previously been proposed by the RSHA to Goering, who had stated then that 'only Hitler could decide', but it was held up by the Interior Ministry, which was nominally in charge of Jewish policy. Heydrich, still smarting from that rejection, had drawn up an interim, scaled-down alternative involving the removal of Jews from the larger German cities. For the moment the redraft was on Hitler's desk, though when he (Hitler) was in the mood he lashed out indignantly that Germany had 'every right' to proceed with expulsions. To circumvent administrative opposition, Heydrich tried another tack, approaching Bormann, who had direct access to the *Führer*.

At a meeting called at short notice by the Propaganda Ministry, those present were asked for proposals to do with the Jewish question that Goebbels could take with him for an audience he was scheduled to have with Hitler. Goebbels's deputy, Leopold Gutterer, attacked the offensive and insolent behaviour of Jews in public. Others described them as enemy spies. 'Identification' was advocated, in itself and also as a prerequisite for further discriminatory measures. Eichmann, mentioning in passing that Heydrich was petitioning Hitler with his revised deportation plan, also made known the existence of the Goering *ermächtigung*. He promised to show it (he never did) to Bernhard Lösener, the representative from the Interior, who, though heavily outnumbered, struggled to reassert the leading position of his department. Lösener, ambushed, was unable to prevent Goebbels from stealing the initiative.

Hitler, recovering by the time Goebbels saw him on 18 August, sounded receptive.[11] Pleased by the handling of the Churchill-Roosevelt summit in the German press, he was heartened that Churchill was still living in the world of 1917 and not 1941. Be that as it may, Hitler was noticeably on edge. In Goebbels's paraphrasing of Hitler's thinking, it was the Jews who would be made to make amends for what they had done. He reminded Goebbels, or Goebbels reminded him, of his pre-war prophecy which was coming true in these weeks and months with uncanny accuracy, making clear how the Jews in the east were having to pay the price, and how the Jews of Germany had already paid in part and would pay still more in the future. He was upping the ante, in other words, to match the moves being made by his transatlantic opponents. On the need for marking he was in full agreement with the introduction of a large visible badge, preparatory to still further steps. He agreed in addition that, as soon as rail transport became available, Berlin's Jews would be 'pushed off' to the east and 'worked over' in the desolate surroundings.

Tobias Jersak believes the publication of the Atlantic Charter signified the final 'encirclement' of Germany, causing Hitler to execute a strategic change of direction. Militarily it meant turning Europe into a German fortress. This military decision, however, was just a 'façade' for a more fundamental racial motivation. Hitler's whole geopolitical strategy was verified by the crystallising, as he now saw it, of his 'fantastical prophecy'.[12] Himmler was already acting on the basis in the eastern territories that 'dead Jews did not need to be deported'. Others were pressing for Berlin's Jews to be carted off to Russia. It was a short step not just to remove the Jews from Germany but also to eliminate them. Jersak's dating is open to challenge. Hitler did appear to consent to an early start with deportation. He then qualified his comments the very next day, repeating the familiar line that it could begin 'once the war is over'. Jersak's assumption that Hitler, at this point in time, decided to have done with the Jews is, to say the least, contentious. But the Charter was a watershed with regard to Hitler's appreciation of the future. He had run a tremendous risk, banking on Russia disintegrating in no more than a few months. A rapid Russian campaign was undertaken so that a war on two fronts would not and could not develop. As Russian resistance stiffened, uneasiness about the outcome began to grow. The US was becoming more and more warlike without actually declaring war. The deterrent – the threat Hitler had delivered in January 1939 – needed strengthening. All of this only *vindicated* his long-held assessment. The war was unwished for, so far as Germany was concerned. The stated intention in the Atlantic Charter – the 'destruction' of the German nation – showed just how great the danger was from the combined forces of 'international Jewry'. It was a blueprint, drawn up in Moscow, London and Washington, for a world Jewish directorate.[13] The challenge must be met blow-for-blow. The Jews had it coming to them for daring to put Germany in such a position.

The accusation that the Jews had 'prepared for, unleashed and were now widening out the extent of the war' was strongly pushed.[14] An article in the Swiss paper *La Gazette de Lausanne* carried details from its Berlin correspondent of reports appearing in the German press, allegedly in response to a speech by Chaim Weizmann, the Zionist leader, and the increasingly hostile actions of the United States, asserting that the Jewish problem, as Jews 'should have known it would be', was being looked into and would be 'definitely' solved, 'as radically as is necessary'.[15] The speculation was, the Swiss paper continued, of a further burst of ghettoisation, involving Germany itself, all German-conquered territory and also 'perhaps' its satellite states.[16] Although rather forced (Weizmann's speech had been given as far back as March) and smacking of bluster, the piece in *La Gazette* lent substance to the idea that a total resolution of the Jewish question was being authoritatively considered, and was expected to be 'radical', both in terms of measures and of geographical extent.

The 'radical' solution adopted in the east was already causing controversy. TASS, the Soviet news agency, announced that German troops were rampaging through villages in the Ukrainian countryside, littering the streets with corpses of women, their children and the elderly. A secret order had been issued, the agency said, telling soldiers to exercise 'ruthlessness against the civilian population'. This material was distributed in turn by the international press. German rebuttals were soon released. The claims were falsehoods, 'Jewish lies', part of a high-level hoax to circulate horror stories, trying to fool Europe in exactly the same way that had been done in the *Weltkrieg*.[17]

The British prime minister then fanned the flames. Intelligence reports based on the interception and decoding of German radio messages indicated that SS and police units in and around Minsk had mopped-up 30,000 civilians, mainly Jews, in just six weeks. Churchill spoke publicly about the 'methodical, merciless butchery' of German 'police-troops' operating on Russian soil, executing 'scores of thousands in cold blood' and exterminating 'whole districts'. He called it 'a crime without a name'.[18]

It is unclear which order – the 'Commissar' or a later one – the Russians had come across. A Soviet offer to observe the rules of the Hague Convention was, in late August, spurned by Hitler. It is also known that Heydrich sent out a missive to the heads of the *Einsatzgruppen* urging greater secrecy, lest any orders should fall into the wrong hands; if there was any risk, paperwork should be returned or incinerated.[19] The head of the order police urged commanders to submit all future reports by courier instead of using radio communication.

Justifying the need for marking German Jews, the German authorities referred instead to Soviet atrocities. Informed by telex of the result of Hitler's talk with Goebbels, Heydrich rushed through a special police regulation 'on behalf of' the Interior Minister, published on 1 September and due to come into force two weeks later. All Jews above the age of six were forbidden to go out without displaying a saucer-sized, solid black six-point star with the inscription 'Jew', to be worn on the left breast.[20] A further provision laid down that they were not to leave their residential area without the written consent of the local police. By segregating the Jewish population they would be dissuaded from appearing in public, the easier to oust them from Germany. The new regulation was announced with an accompanying note prepared for the press, explaining that the German people would not have to come into unwanted contact with Jews, who up to that point had been able to camouflage their presence. It added for good measure that the Soviet secret police-led Jewish policy of annihilating other free peoples in the east had been clearly evident to every German soldier.[21] Bormann applied his own touch, putting into circulation the fabrication that German citizens in the United States were being made to wear Swastika emblems.

The pressure to deport was building up. It was relevant not just to the distant aim of population transfer and Germanisation. It would have an immediate value, purging the Reich of a troublesome minority that was seditiously working for Germany's defeat; it might intimidate other disruptive groups too. The war had been willed by Jewish fanatics, who were now doing everything they could to prolong the carnage, trying to spread turmoil inside and outside the Reich.[22] Goebbels advocated 'a gradual cutting off of all possibilities'.[23] Himmler obliged, bringing in an emigration ban on German Jews between the ages of 18 and 45, news of which only seeped out in the succeeding weeks. Officially it was ascribed to the 'labour shortage'.[24] In his weekly editorial in *Das Reich*, Goebbels implored his readers to stand firm and not to listen to enemy broadcasters who must not be allowed to sow discord and divide Germany all over again. As for the 'Communist Jews', they would not be able to 'escape' a just penalty. 'Await the hour.'[25]

Notes

1. *Kleine Volks-Zeitung*, 29 July 1941.
2. E. Fröhlich (ed.), *Die Tagebücher von Joseph Goebbels* (Munich: K.G. Saur, 1996), II, 1, entry dated 24 July 1941.
3. T. Sandkühler, *'Endlösung' in Galizien: der Judenmord in Ostpolen und die Rettungsinitiativen von Berthold Beitz 1941–1944* (Bonn: Dietz, 1996), p.113.
4. *BBC Monitoring Report* No.746, 2-3 August 1941 (Daily Digest covering Germany and German-controlled stations).
5. See Alex J. Kay's handling of these points in his 'Transition to Genocide, July 1941: Einsatzkommando 9 and the Annihilation of Soviet Jewry', *Holocaust and Genocide Studies*, 27, 3 (Winter 2013), pp.411-42.
6. H. Trevor-Roper (ed.), *Hitler's Table Talk* (London: Weidenfeld and Nicolson, 1953), entry dated 11-12 July 1941.

7. W. Lower, *Nazi Empire-Building and the Holocaust in Ukraine* (Chapel Hill, NC: University of North Carolina Press, 2005).

8. N. Terry, 'Conflicting Signals: British Intelligence on the "Final Solution" through Radio Intercepts and Other Sources, 1941-1942', in *Yad Vashem Studies*, XXXII (2003), p.355.

9. T4 was a 'mercy killing' operation authorised by Hitler in October 1939, permitting physicians to end the lives of those (the handicapped, the incurably ill, the economically burdensome) deemed to be 'unworthy of living'. It was run from an office attached to the Reich Chancellery in Berlin.

10. K. Schleunes (ed.), *Legislating the Holocaust – the Bernhard Loesener memoirs* (Boulder, CO: Westview, 2001), p.79. Lösener, at some personal risk, kept copies of his own departmental memoranda.

11. See Fröhlich (ed.), *Die Tagebücher von Joseph Goebbels*, entry dated 19 August 1941.

12. T. Jersak, 'Die Interaktion von Kriegsverlauf und Judenvernichtung: ein Blick auf Hitler's Strategie im Spätsommer 1941' in *Historische Zeitschrift*, 268 (April 1999), pp.311-74.

13. *Völkischer Beobachter*, 17 August 1941; *Berliner Börsen-Zeitung*, 20 August 1941.

14. *Völkischer Beobachter*, 22 August 1941.

15. The source was in turn an article in the *Berliner Börsen-Zeitung* of 22 August 1941.

16. *La Gazette de Lausanne*, 23 August 1941. Germany itself never had any ghettos.

17. *Berliner Börsen-Zeitung*, 21 August 1941.

18. *The Times*, 25 August 1941.

19. W. Benz, K. Kwiet and J. Matthäus (eds), *Einsatz im 'Reichskommissariat Ostland'* (Berlin: Metropol, 1998), p.67.

20. *Deutsches Reichsgesetzblatt*, I (1941), Number 100, p.547.

21. *Wiener Kronen-Zeitung*, 13 September 1941.

22. At a press conference in Moscow, a group of Soviet intellectuals pleaded for Jews around the world to do everything in their power to wreck the German economy by boycotting German goods and disrupting its vital industries. They preached the gospel of solidarity with the Soviet Union in its fight against 'the enemy of mankind'. Unless the Nazis were defeated, they cautioned, extrapolating from the suffering already occurring in Soviet lands, 'wholesale extermination will be the lot of all Jews, including those in the United States and Britain'.

23. See Fröhlich (ed.), *Die Tagebücher von Joseph Goebbels*, entry dated 26 August 1941.

24. According to the 'reliably' informed *The New York Times*, 2 September 1941.

25. An extract was carried in *Neue Warte am Inn*, 27 August 1941.

6

'The Greatest Crime'

The faltering momentum of the German advance coincided with a new spirit of unruliness taking hold in other parts of Hitler's Europe, a spirit that the Anglo-American Atlantic Charter looked to nurture. The German army was losing its aura of invincibility. Along with the steadily rising tally in the dead and wounded on the eastern front, a dozen or so divisions were tied up elsewhere, such as in the Balkans, where the army's control was precarious. Underground cells were flourishing even in western Europe. All of this was impairing Germany's ability to wage war.

Hitler believed he was his own best commander. He had, as he often reminded his generals, fought as a frontline soldier and understood combat at close quarters. He was also convinced, as a one-time revolutionary, that he knew what it took to stamp out the threat of 'fifth columnists' and other 'sinister forces'. He had made a special study of the weaknesses of the multi-ethnic Hapsburg monarchy.[1] In the occupied east, since no regard need be paid to the Hague Convention, trust was put in the application of brute, often deadly force. Keitel, on Hitler's orders, underlined this with a High Command edict urging that 'the fight against Bolshevism necessitates indiscriminate accomplishment of this task, especially also against the Jews, the main carriers of Bolshevism'.[2] But in the west, too, though they were more exposed to the eyes of the outside world, Hitler demanded a 'mailed fist'. He had raised this with Marshal Kvaternik in July, grumbling about the curse of 'asocials' and 'parasites', and it continued to preoccupy him throughout August and early September, always linking criminal opposition with Jewish or Jewish-inspired manoeuvres.

Occupying officials were struggling to contain the number of disorders. In Norway a state of emergency had to be introduced as a result of 'disruption' by 'Communist and Marxist elements' in the trade unions. The Dutch population set up a campaign of passive opposition and non-cooperation. In France, in response to repeated attacks on German troops, the French police rounded up some 4,000 male Jews, many of them foreign-born, who were taken to internment camps. Serbia was in open revolt, stoked by Russian irregulars and 'Jewish communists'. When the German

Foreign Office official, Franz Rademacher, asked Eichmann about the possibility of expelling 1,200 Serbian Jews to the *General Gouvernement* or Russia, Eichmann's advice was to shoot them out of hand.

Eventually a directive was despatched on 16 September to military commanders in European capitals setting out guidelines for countering 'banditry'.[3] The wording was stark. 'Communist insurrections' had, since the beginning of the Russian conflict, broken out in all parts of German-occupied territory on a 'mass' scale, orchestrated from Moscow and endangering, to an increasing extent, the conduct of the war. To quell this insurrectionary movement it was vital to clamp down with the 'harshest methods' at the first sign of trouble, nipping it in the bud. The death penalty must be imposed on 50 to 100 Communists for every murdered German soldier, as well as in cases before the courts involving espionage, sabotage and the illegal possession of weapons. A draconian riposte was unavoidable, Keitel acknowledged, before they lost all capacity to cope.

Hitler's greatest fear was that organised unrest would spread to the Reich itself. His regime was structured to stifle dissent and prevent the kind of descent into anarchy that had been Germany's downfall in the Great War. To discourage 'new sources of agitation', he was willing to go to 'the last extremity'.[4] All that was needed was one more overwhelming blow to put an end to the efforts of those trying to hold up an irresistible German triumph.

In spite of dogged Soviet skirmishing, Kiev was about to fall and Moscow was confidently expected to follow with the unleashing of Operation Typhoon. Anticipating a final resolution within the next two to three weeks, Hitler took two major decisions. The first was to overrule his senior naval staff and refrain from initiating any aggressive actions in the Atlantic that could provide Roosevelt with an excuse to declare war. The United States must be kept out of the conflict until victory in Russia was assured.[5] The second decision – after intense lobbying by Goebbels and others – was to recommence the deportation of German Jewry without in fact waiting until the cessation of hostilities.

The order to deport Germany's remaining 170,000 Jews had been discussed by Hitler, Himmler and (it appears) Ribbentrop, in a series of conversations at Rastenburg. Reconstructing exactly what passed between them involves a good deal of guesswork. Once more we have to rely on a single, terse document. In a letter to Arthur Greiser, Gauleiter of the Warthegau, Himmler communicated 'the *Führer's* wish' that the old German Reich and the Protectorate of Bohemia and Moravia were to be emptied of all Jews as soon as practicable and, if possible, 'by this year'. Himmler said he understood from preliminary enquiries that the ghetto of

Lodz – renamed Litzmannstadt – in Greiser's province was in a position to accommodate an initial 60,000 for the winter before being sent on 'to the east' in the spring. He asked Greiser to do everything in his power to assist with a step that was in the interests of the whole of Greater Germany.[6]

It is Hitler's categorical change of mind, rather than the mildness of Himmler's choice of words, which is so glaring. He was ordering a substantial clear-out, beginning in but not limited to Berlin, Vienna and Prague and therefore going much further than Heydrich's latest proposal. There was, too, the additional emphasis on urgency. The general sense was that, so far as the Reich's Jews were concerned, he was sealing their fate. Senior Nazis boasted that soon there would not be any Jews left in Germany. The savage Bormann, talking to foreign correspondents while gulping down champagne in Berlin's *Kaiserhof* hotel, said he had given his word he would carry out his master's order.[7] The press echoed this feeling, one paper suggesting the moment had come 'to rid the world of this evil'.[8]

Why the sudden hurry? What had altered?

Hitler's two decisions are more accurately viewed as two components of one and the same decision. The defeat of the Soviets was surely at hand. After clashes between US naval and merchant shipping and German U-boats, Roosevelt had just introduced a 'shoot-on-sight' order to protect the convoys crossing the Atlantic to the British Isles, some of their cargo also being transported onwards by the northern sea route to Russia. Although Roosevelt's announcement was a blatant act of war in the eyes of the German Foreign Office, Hitler was unwilling to provide the American President with an incident he could use as a *casus belli*. Even so, the United States was edging closer to an outright state of armed conflict with every passing week. Restarting the deportation of Germany's Jews was a proportionate way of indicating that American activism was going to be costly and that the cost – in lives – would steadily rise.

There were other considerations which may plausibly have been behind the timing. The Soviets had transported the entire German population of the Volga region to Siberia. Rosenberg had proposed they should 'make the Jews of Central Europe suffer for it' by packing them off to his eastern territories, an idea that briefly interested Hitler, though he let it be known, clearly in line with his 'tit-for-tat' stratagem, that he was reserving this ultimate option for actual American entry.[9] The German Ambassador to France, Otto Abetz, speaking with Himmler on 16 September, put the case for deporting Jews from occupied France; when he saw Hitler shortly afterwards, Hitler ruled out any changes in policy towards the French until the war in the east was 'wound up', but Abetz listened to him indulging in 'exterminationist fantasies' about 'obliterating' the 'Asiatics' and 'Bolsheviks'.[10] Reports were also coming in from Hamburg, a city that was being subjected to heavy aerial bombing (the strategic equivalent to the blockading of Germany in the Great War). Jewish occupants were being evicted from their homes in retaliation and the provincial Gauleiters asked for them to be evacuated.

One further factor, however, suggests how much was at stake. While Himmler was writing to Greiser, Heydrich had sent a draft decree to Lammers about a matter which, he said, was currently greatly exercising Hitler: the security of the Reich. Heydrich drew attention to several challenges facing the regime – growing cross-border infiltration, the activity of enemy agents, political subversion and 'the fight against international criminality' – which were not being adequately addressed by the existing organisational set-up. He wanted the RSHA's policing powers to be enlarged to the rest of the German sphere of influence. At one with Heydrich's application, and as propagandists were claiming, the obvious support the Jews were giving to 'illegal' resistance had 'certainly not been overlooked'.[11]

This is borne out by an appraisal of events in the Protectorate of Bohemia and Moravia, where some 90,000 Jews were, in accordance with the *Führer's* 'wish', earmarked for expulsion.

Czechoslovakia had been the first of Hitler's hostile takeovers. The Czech half, though mainly non-German speaking, was still thought of as fit for Germanising. A puppet government served under the Reich Protector, Konstantin von Neurath, and his ambitious deputy Karl Hermann Frank. While von Neurath was in office, efforts to assimilate the Czechs were relatively restrained, and his biographer believes von Neurath was 'satisfied' by Hitler's standing instruction that all schemes for deportation were put off for the duration of the war.[12]

German expansion into south-eastern Europe in the spring of 1941 and the subsequent invasion of the Soviet Union had a notable effect upon the Protectorate. Its heavy industries had already been converted to arms manufacture, particularly of aircraft, tanks and artillery, supplying the German army's huge demands. It was additionally a transport hub of the rail network for troop movements to and from the east. The Czechs, however, were reluctant anti-Bolsheviks, many of them hoping the Red Army could help restore their Slavic independence. In July there was an outbreak of short strikes and wrecking of machinery, fuelled by resentment at the scarcity of food. In early August demonstrators protested about anti-Jewish legislation. Frank, dismayed by von Neurath's leniency, wanted to tighten prohibitions on Jews in public places and advocated marking, which von Neurath agreed to, and this came into force at the same time as in Germany proper. Czechs who chose to wear a Star of David as an expression of support were chastised for their 'scandalous' behaviour. The German-language newspapers talked of 'an ever-growing hatred' which was making the situation intolerable. According to the Swedish Consul in Prague, it was like sitting 'on a volcano'.[13]

The finger of blame was pointed at the Czechoslovakian government-in-exile in London, which maintained secret links as well as broadcasting over the English radio. Some success had already been achieved with the 'Victory in Europe' or 'V' campaign. Speakers began encouraging people to go slow at work and to boycott the Czech newspapers. Increasing interference with troop and goods trains, arson and explosions in key factories and unexplained industrial accidents led to declining industrial output. When von Neurath forwarded his usual monthly report on 15 September, he raised the alarm. The Czechs, outwardly cooperative but emboldened by the feeling that Germany would lose the war, were doing all they could to hinder production. In working-class districts the deterioration in food supplies was causing widespread discontent and there were stoppages of work, even in war-related enterprises. Further strikes were likely, especially a general strike on the day of national independence (28 October). Despite police measures against the ring leaders, enemy propaganda encouraging disobedience was 'extraordinarily effective'. The impact of the supply shortages on the political outlook was 'extremely serious'. Von Neurath asked Lammers to 'speedily' bring his report to Hitler's notice.[14]

The crisis came to a head that same evening. In Prague there were street battles between protestors and the occupying forces, with many dead and wounded. The security police cordoned off the city and martial law was invoked. At an emergency meeting on the 16th, Frank is supposed to have called for tougher counter-measures. Von Neurath declined, whereupon Frank decided to go behind von Neurath's back and request an interview with Hitler.

Incoming reports from other security organs played on Hitler's misgivings about the loyalty of the Czechs, who were sabotaging the military effort at the worst possible moment. The absolute necessity was to prevent the contagion from spreading. Himmler had given him an assurance that imprisoned opponents would be eliminated if troubles were to arise 'at home'. As Hitler put it, talking of the Czech insurgency, the betrayal in the rear of an army fighting at the front was 'the greatest crime'.[15] The Jews were working for 'the other side'. It was them or us. They must go.

Von Neurath and Frank were both brought before Hitler, who had Frank's report to hand. Manufacturing was estimated to have fallen by 20 to 30 per cent. The position was bad and bound to become worse. A 'sharper course' was required. To von Neurath's surprise, Hitler (possibly swayed by Bormann) told him he was replacing him for the time being with Heydrich. 'The Reich is in danger.' Heydrich would not scruple to act. Stabilising the Protectorate included driving forward the deportation process.[16] 'The Jews in London' were put on notice. They were the ones inspiring the Czech population to defy their masters. If this were to continue, 'it would be necessary to consider reprisals against Protectorate Jews.'[17]

From the moment he was installed on 29 September, Heydrich set his sights on restoring 'calm and order'. The head of the government, General Elias, was arrested and interrogated. Hundreds of other ex-army officers, civil servants and businessmen were taken into custody. Executions were carried out. Martial law was extended to much of the rest of the country. Radios were confiscated. The press printed details of law-breaking Jews who, hand-in-hand with the Communists, were controlling all the tendencies directed against the Reich. A 'complete, unconditional and iron-hard break with Judaism' was necessary for the whole nation.[18]

Heydrich outlined his intentions in a speech to his staff. The past few weeks had seen 'terroristic' actions on a large scale, seeking to push the country to the point of rebellion, seriously harming arms production and providing an example to other parts of German-occupied territory which could not be allowed – in short, a 'stab-in-the-back'. Their task was to firmly prevent all further interruptions to the economy, but it could not be done only by coercion. Rations would be improved. In the longer run, because the Czech lands had always been the origin of 'dagger blows' against Germany, they would be absorbed into the Reich. Those of 'good race' were acceptable. The racially inferior and the hostile 'are to be got rid of. There is lots of space in the east for them.'

He proceeded by degrees. He began by ending any exemptions to the wearing of a Star of David. This was followed up by the closure of all synagogues – centres of 'whispering campaigns' – and a curb on black marketeering. Finally, editors of the leading newspapers were directed to call for the removal of Jews from the major cities.

Analysis of the daily press helps to isolate the basic themes. The Jews were bringing it upon themselves. They were responsible for the political upheaval and economic illegality afflicting the Protectorate. They were the rallying point for all subversive elements, taking their cue from London, dividing the Czech nation and poisoning German-Czech relations. But they were mistaken if they thought they could do what they had done before. The current war was very different to the one in 1914-18. Germany was 'cleansing' the body politic. The 'discarding' – totally and quickly – of the Jews would advance 'to a very high pitch the Final Solution of the Jewish Question in the Protectorate'.[19]

These unsettling events were not yet reported on in any depth in Germany.[20] Hitler had not spoken publicly since the launching of Barbarossa. On the eve of what was meant to be the final assault on Moscow, he issued an Order of the Day to his troops, pointing out how defeating the Russians would remove England's last ally in Europe and that all that stood between Germany and one of 'the most tremendous victories in history' were 'Jews and only Jews'. Returning to Berlin, he arrived – flanked by Heydrich[21] – at the *Sportpalast* to address the nation. The Russian fighting machine, he acknowledged, had been underestimated. But this only reinforced his belief that it had been necessary to attack Russia pre-emptively. For the first time he committed himself to saying that the Bolshevik enemy was 'broken' and the war was nearing its end. The military front and the home front were uniting in 'a single community of sacrifice', solidified by the move to drive out all of those destabilising elements which were in league with Germany's international enemies.

Notes

1.   W. Görlitz (ed.), *The Memoirs of Field-Marshal Keitel* (London: Kimber, 1965), pp.144-5 and 152-3.
2.   'Jews in the newly occupied eastern territories' (Document 878-PS of 12 September 1941), in *Nazi Conspiracy and Aggression*, III (1946), p.636.
3.   *Documents on German Foreign Policy*, D, XIII (Washington, DC: US Government Printing Office, 1954), pp.541-3.
4.   *Le Journal de Genève*, 2 September 1941.
5.   *Führer Conferences on Naval Affairs* (Annapolis, MD: Naval Institute Press, 1990), report of 17 September 1941, pp.231-5.
6.   P. Witte, 'Two Decisions Concerning the "Final Solution to the Jewish Question": Deportations to Lodz and Mass Murder in Chelmno', in *Holocaust and Genocide Studies*, 9, 3 (Winter 1995), p.330.
7.   P. Huss, *The Foe We Face* (Garden City, NY: Doubleday, Doran and Co, 1942), pp.243 and 248. Huss was the chief correspondent of the (American) International News Service in Berlin until his departure in November 1941.
8.   *Das Kleine Blatt*, 1 October 1941.
9.   According to the diary of Walter Koeppen, quoted in P. Longerich, *Holocaust: The Nazi Persecution and Murder of the Jews* (Oxford: Oxford University Press, 2010), p.268.

10. *Documents on German Foreign Policy 1918-1945*, D, XIII (Washington, DC: US Government Printing Office, 1954), pp.518-20.

11. *Der Südostdeutsche Tageszeitung*, 20 September 1941.

12. J. Heinemann, *Hitler's First Foreign Minister – Constantin Freiherr von Neurath* (Los Angeles, CA: University of California Press, 1979), p.208.

13. A. Suppan, *Hitler-Benes-Tito* (Vienna: Austrian Academy of Sciences Press, 2014), 2, p.811.

14. M.Karny et al (eds), *Deutsche Politikim 'Protektorat Böhmen Und Mähren' unter Reinhard Heydrich 1941-1942: Eine Dokumentation* (Berlin: Metropol, 1997), document number 1 dated 15 September 1941.

15. H.D. Heilman, 'Aus dem Kriegstagebuch des Diplomaten Otto Bräutigam – Wiedergabe des Textes mit einem ausführlichen kommentierenden Anhang, in G. Aly et al (eds), *Biedermann und Schreibtischtäter* (Berlin: Rotbuch Verlag, 1987), entry dated 30 September 1941.

16. R. Gerwarth, *Hitler's Hangman – The Life of Heydrich* (New Haven, CT: Yale University Press, 2011), pp.223-5.

17. *Prager Abend*, 25 September 1941, in the Jewish Telegraphic Agency news bulletin, 26 September 1941.

18. *Lidove Noviny*, 1 October 1941.

19. *Ceske Slovo*, 5 October 1941; *Lidove Noviny*, 6 October 1941; *Venkov*, 14 October 1941.

20. Major articles did not appear until the end of the month (e.g. a lengthy comment in the *Neues Wiener Tagblatt* on 30 October commending the 'promptness' of Germany's 'punitive measures').

21. *The Telegraph* (Brisbane), 6 October 1941, quoting Czech sources in London.

7

Three 'Solutions'

Hitler's injunction to Himmler to clear the Reich of all Jews 'as soon as practicable' was driven by a clear political imperative – neutralising the Jewish danger by rapid evacuation. Although victory was within sight and Himmler and Heydrich had begun to think in concrete terms about eventually consigning German Jewry to some of the frozen outposts of the Soviet 'GULAG' prison complex[1], the intention preceded any ideas about where in the short term they were going to go. The rush to fulfil Hitler's demand was largely what shaped the provisional nature of the arrangements which emerged.

Chelmno

Himmler had already been to Posen to see Greiser, presumably to obtain his prior agreement to a substantial influx of Jews into the ghetto in Lodz. Greiser was at first unwilling. 145,000 people were crammed into a closely guarded, four square kilometre section of the old town. For eighteen months he had been trying to shunt them onwards into the neighbouring *General Gouvernement*. Hans Frank's refusal had Hitler's backing. Himmler was now expecting Greiser to accept many more. Snatches of the correspondence provide a good picture of the awkward haggling which ensued. Eichmann, as Heydrich's envoy, went to Lodz to negotiate. He sought to bounce the local governor, Friedrich Übelhör, into agreeing by asserting that the ghetto administrator had given his assent. Übelhör objected, claiming Eichmann was using phony figures. Eventually the latter consented to take in a total of 20,000, one-third of what Himmler had been asking for, topped up by a further 5,000 Gypsies, but he protested to Himmler about Eichmann's underhand methods. Himmler, in reply, criticized Übelhör's objectionable and insubordinate attitude. Once the deal was struck, Eichmann presented the Ministry of the Interior with a *fait accompli*. When the army's Chief Quartermaster pressed for the newcomers 'from air raid-endangered areas' to go elsewhere, Himmler's overruled him, insisting the action had nothing to do with air raids but was being taken for 'fundamental reasons'.[2]

Ian Kershaw's groundbreaking lecture on 'improvised genocide' in the Warthegau uncovered the transactions which evidently took place.[3] Greiser accepted a (smaller) total in return for the freedom to 'reduce' the ghetto by other means. Led by Dr Viktor Brack from Hitler's Private Chancellery, a special commando team made up of members of the disbanded T4 euthanasia unit was detailed to find a suitable site for the experimental gassing of victims, using a specially adapted coach which piped the exhaust into an airtight compartment in the rear. The chosen site was an old manor house in the village of Chelmno, 50 kilometres to the north of Lodz. Greiser, with the direct empowerment of Hitler[4], was a party to a compromise which stemmed from a local, civilian arrangement to address the Jewish issue in his territory.

It followed from these exchanges that the incoming German Jews might not be moved on in the spring. Indirect recognition of this appeared in the text of a speech that Greiser gave in November, obtained by the Swedish newspaper, *Dagens Nyheter*.[5] He designated the Warthegau a training ground for all of eastern Europe. One of the most important tasks was the fight against the Jews. He was 'solving' the problem not by chasing them away, as was being done elsewhere, but by putting them to work under strong management. In the Lodz ghetto they were toiling for their livelihood. The broad hint was that they were useful only if and as long as they were economically productive.

Riga and Minsk

Since Lodz could not and would not receive larger numbers, it fell to Eichmann to search for alternatives. He had to fend off inquirers, telling them he did not know when circumstances would change. One person he contacted was the head of the *Einsatzgruppe* in the *Ostland*, Walter Stahlecker, an old Austrian acquaintance. The idea they came up with was to arrange for the construction of camps in Riga and Minsk, purpose-built to accommodate up to 50,000 inmates. As a first step, since time was short, 5,000 could go to camps built by the Russians to house political detainees, presently in the combat zone occupied by two other *Einsatz* commanders. At one stroke, Eichmann's difficulty was eased and the RSHA could stick to a starting date of mid-October. At lunch on the 6th, Hitler was informing the new military plenipotentiary in Prague, General Toussaint, that the Jews in the Protectorate – the main 'transmission belt' of enemy news to the

Czech populace – were not going at first to the *General Gouvernement* but immediately to the east.[6] Heydrich held an official meeting in Prague on the 10th, just prior to a press conference. Admitting he had had to respect the views of the administration in Lodz, he went on to unveil Eichmann's initiative, stressing that the priority was to remove the 'most burdensome' Jews. The rest would be housed in the old Czech fortress town of Theresienstadt which would act as a temporary collection camp. 'The *Fuhrer* wishes' to empty the German space of Jews by the year's end, he reiterated. It was incumbent upon them to make haste, resolving all outstanding questions.[7]

As had happened with the Nisko fiasco, Eichmann was characteristically callous, intent on offloading his charges without much ado. Deposited where the Commissar Order was still in force, the German Jews would be wholly unprotected. Then again, an administrative distinction was still being made between Jews of the *Altreich* and the *Ostjuden*. Stahlecker, quoting Hitler's authority, instructed the commander of the security police in Latvia, Rudolf Lange, to alter a projected camp for Rigan Jews to be built at Salaspils, not far from Riga, so that it could be used instead for Jews from Germany.

The Ministry for the Occupied Eastern Territories was a disobliging ally, however. Rosenberg, the Minister, would not – despite Hitler's ruling in July – give ground to Himmler on the policing issue. Rosenberg was irked by Himmler's habit of travelling to the front and dishing out orders face-to-face. Heydrich was equally irritated by the obstructiveness of Rosenberg's secretary of state, Alfred Meyer, admonishing him for not doing enough to weed out so many supposedly 'indispensable' Jewish workers, whose retention was 'nullifying' the plan for the total eviction of all Jews from the occupied eastern area. The Jewish question was in every respect 'in the hands of the security police' and he threatened to hold further discussions.[8]

Rosenberg, given the 'make the Jews suffer for it' proposition he had put to Hitler in September, must at least have agreed to allow the Jewish transports to Riga and Minsk. The *Reichskommissar* for the *Ostland*, Hinrich Lohse, was not so easily assuaged. Lohse, to create a *judenfrei* Baltic, was herding Jews into a handful of new ghettos (the largest of them, Riga, had 25,000 occupants) which he wanted to preserve for their economic worth – the very thing Heydrich was losing his patience about. The barbarous manner in which Jewish women and children were disposed of in Liepaja by Stahlecker's men caused 'general consternation', and Lohse forbade any further shootings. Stahlecker complained in a report to Heydrich, who decided to ask the *Ostministerium* for an explanation. In the meantime Lohse had heard about the forthcoming arrival of thousands of German Jews and made his way back to Berlin to express his disapproval in person.

Lohse's clashes with Stahlecker resulted in the production of another essential text in Holocaust history, the often-cited 'Wetzel' letter. It was a typewritten draft with pencilled corrections attributed to Dr Erhard Wetzel, a jurist who had recently joined the Eastern Ministry as an adviser on racial affairs.[9] He was replying on behalf of Rosenberg to a somewhat cryptic enquiry concerning 'the solution of the Jewish question' from Lohse on 4 October. Wetzel wrote to say that he had been in touch with *Oberdienstleiter* Brack of the Reich Chancellery, who was ready to collaborate in manufacturing the necessary 'shelters' and 'gassing apparatus'. Brack would send his chemicals expert, a Dr Kallmeyer, to Riga to construct them up there. *Sturmbannführer* Eichmann, 'the *referat* on Jewish matters in the RSHA' whom Wetzel had also seen, 'is in agreement with this process'. According to Eichmann, Wetzel said, 'camps for Jews are to be set up in Riga and Minsk to which Jews from the *Altreich* may possibly be sent. At the present time Jews being deported from the *Altreich* are being sent to Litzmannstadt [Lodz], but also to other camps, to be later used as labour in the East in so far as they are capable of work.' Wetzel added a second paragraph:

> As the affairs now stand, there are no objections against doing away with those Jews who are not able to work, with the Brack remedy. In this way, occurrences such as those which, according to a report presently before me, took place at the shooting of Jews in Wilna [Vilno] and which, considering that the shootings were public, were hardly excusable, would no longer be possible. Those able to work, on the other hand, will be transported to the East for labor [sic] service. It is self-understood that among the Jews capable of work, men and women are to be kept separate.[10]

It is a startling memorandum which Eichmann, on one occasion, called an authentic record. The gassing of unproductive Jews in the *Ostland*, Lohse was being told, was officially acceptable. Gassing would avoid the grisly scenes that had upset him. German Jews might shortly arrive. The unproductive ones among them could be treated in a corresponding way.[11] This was 'the (recommended) solution'.

The unanswered point is what was in Lohse's letter of 4 October. His personal papers, found by British intelligence officers behind a false wall in the castle of Plön in July 1945, strangely disappeared. After the war, because of his falling out with Stahlecker, he was able to present himself as an opponent of Jewish persecution. Luckily the point was cleared up by Otto Bräutigam, Wetzel's departmental head, in an interrogation in 1948, though it has never before been published.

> A: '...I can remember the following. *Reichskommissar* Lohse reported in the course of the summer [sic] of 1941 that the liquidation of the Jews was being carried out in his *Reichskommissariat,* often in a cruel way, and he asked the Eastern Ministry to ensure that gas vans were sent to his *Reichskommissariat* for this purpose. I was at the time with the OKH [the Army High Command] and was in the Ministry for a couple of days and they showed me the report. He used the phrase 'euthanasia vans'. We racked our brains about what these were. He gave a name, a single syllable name, of someone in the Reich Chancellery, who was responsible for this thing.
> Q: Can you not remember the name?
> A: No, I only read it the one time, but he must be known of here. If I hear it again, I'll know it. I think I've read about him in the newspapers.[12]

Bräutigam's recollection fills in a great deal, establishing that the proposition to use gas vans came from Lohse, who already knew about Brack's activities. In other words, like in the case of Lodz, it was a local response to problems associated with the anticipated arrival of Jewish deportees. Shooting of the uneconomic could be replaced by gassing, which was not so crude and also a lot less public. A gas van did in fact appear in Riga in December.[13]

Lublin

Another possible course of action was to revive deportations (halted in March 1941) to Lublin, the easterly outpost of the *General Gouvernement.* The presiding Higher SS and Police leader, Odilo Globocnik[14], allocated by Himmler with numerous assignments, operated with a considerable degree of independence. Lublin town was, historically, a nucleus of Jewish trade and learning. His primary job was to transform it into the central pillar in a network of eastern strong points of the Greater Germany-to-come, gradually squeezing out the Polish and Jewish natives. He had instituted a complex of Jewish workshops busily producing equipment for the front, putting the Jews to work, under Jewish supervision, as the best way of counteracting their 'harmful' habits – and filling his own pockets. Ghettoised and subject to a growing range of prohibitions, Lublin's Jews were slowly being isolated from their neighbouring Poles. In the early stages, it was a point for self-congratulation on Globocnik's part that the Germans were not, 'unlike other colonial powers', resorting either directly or indirectly to '*vernichtungsaktionen*' (extermination).[15]

But Lublin, too, had links to the T4 euthanasia team. Philip Bouhler (head of the Reich Chancellery) and his assistant, Brack, are thought to have called on Globocnik in September 1941, discussing the deportation programme that was shortly to begin. Frank, however, would not budge, personally revoking an order by Heydrich for two trainloads of Jews from Hamburg to proceed to Lublin in early October. For now, however, Globocnik was 'concentrating' the ethnic Germans and forcibly displacing 'foreign nationals' and asked for the *Reichsführer's* permission to press ahead with the job of 'completely kicking out the Jews'.[16] To bolster his case he made much of the importance of pacifying the region. Impressed by this 'bold and forward thinking', Himmler registered his approval. The Lublin ghetto was accordingly reorganized and the system of work permits rationalized with a view to the 'gradual cleansing' of the local Jewish population, thereby making room for resettled Jews from the Reich.

It is likely that a decision was made at about the same time to set up a fixed, rather than mobile, gassing facility. A delegation of senior SS officers and specialists, 'led' by Eichmann, is believed to have visited Belzec, a small village in a forested area 75 kilometres to the south-east of Lublin, next to the railway line to Lvov (Lemberg).[17] They carefully examined the neighbourhood, which had some bunkers and a power plant left behind by the Soviets, and considered the technical, engineering and transportation options concerning the adoption of 'special measures'. In early November work on the site in Belzec began.

These small-scale solutions add up to a confused if not chaotic picture. There was clearly some central direction given the sudden prospect of extreme overcrowding. But was there enough to support the contention that the deportation decision was synonymous with a wider determination to finish off the Jews and that the apparent lack of co-ordination was due to the time it took for officials lower down the hierarchy to work out what could be done? Or was the muddle symptomatic of the *absence* of any settled directive from above? Each 'solution' – in trying to overcome dissatisfaction with shooting the 'unwanted' and 'worthless' by bullet – was localised and limited. Each, while solving matters in its own way, was offered as a model for others to copy. Each of the killing sites and killing methods also involved the T4 organisation, but it was the ubiquitous Eichmann who was the diligent linkman.

Notes

1. G. Aly, *Endlösung – Völkerverschiebung und der Mord an den europäischen Juden* (Frankfurt a. M.: Fischer Verlag, 1998), pp.273-4, and N. Wachsmann's chapter, 'The Nazi Concentration Camps in International Context', in J. Rüger and N. Wachsmann (eds), *Rewriting German History – New Perspectives on Modern Germany* (Basingstoke: Palgrave Macmillan, 2015), pp.317-8.
2. The Lodz ghetto specialised in textile production, such as uniforms for the armed forces. Facsimiles of the exchange of letters are reproduced in P. Klein, *Marketing und Massenmord – Die 'Gettoverwaltung Litzmannstadt' 1940-1944* (2008), p.8.
3. I. Kershaw, 'Improvised Genocide? The Emergence of the "Final Solution" in the "Warthegau"', in *Transactions of the Royal Historical Society*, 2 (Cambridge: Cambridge University Press, 1992), pp.51-78.
4. The senior SS and Police chief in the Warthegau, Wilhelm Koppe, claimed Greiser had given him to understand it was an order from the Führer. See the extract from his post-war testimony reprinted in E. Kogon et al, *Les Chambres à Gaz – Secret d'Etat* (Paris: Minuit, 1984), p.100. Peter Klein suggests this empowerment took place on 18 July 1941, when Greiser saw Hitler at Rastenburg (*Die 'Gettoverwaltung Litzmannstadt' 1940 bis 1944* (Hamburg: Hamburger Edition, 2009), pp.346-7. Catherine Epstein, the biographer of Greiser (*Model Nazi – Arthur Greiser and the Occupation of Western Poland* (Oxford: Oxford University Press, 2012)), is not so sure.
5. *Dagens Nyheter*, 23 November 1941.
6. The diary of Werner Koeppen, quoted in M.Karny et al (eds), *Deutsche Politik im 'Protektorat Böhmen Und Mähren' unter Reinhard Heydrich 1941-1942: Eine Dokumentation* (Berlin: Metropol, 1997), p.130.
7. 'Notizen aus der Besprechung am 10.10.41 über die Lösung von Judenfragen', Yad Vashem Archives, TR.3, File 1193. Accessed on 12 February 2021 from: https://documents.yadvashem.org.
8. 'Niederschrift einer Besprechung zwischen Heydrich, Gauleiter Meyer et al vom 4.10.1941', in B. Hoppe and H. Glass, *Die Verfolgung und Ermordung der europäischen Juden durch das nationalsozialistische Deutschland*, 7 (Munich: Oldenbourg, 2011), pp.550-3.
9. The letter was never sent.
10. Translation of the Wetzel draft prepared for the Office of the US Chief Counsel at Nuremberg in the Nuremberg Trials Project archive. Accessed on 12 February 2021 from: https://nuremberg.law.harvard.edu/documents/1676-draft-of-letter-to-the-reich?q=wetzel#p.1). Claude Lanzmann, filming his epic *Shoah*, tried – fruitlessly – to locate the elderly Wetzel in the 1970s.
11. Florent Brayard challenges this inference, arguing that the *Ostjuden* and the *Westjuden* were to be treated differently.

12. *US National Archives, M1019 – Records of the U.S. Nuernberg War Crimes Trials Interrogations* (1946-1949), Interrogation Report No.2636a, 6 February 1948, pp.1-2 (Courtesy of the Hoover Institution Library, Stanford University). Brack was tried at Nuremberg in 1946-47 and hung in June 1948.

13. M. Beer, 'Die Entwicklung der Gaswagen beim Mord an den Juden', in *Vierteljahrshefte für Zeitgeschichte,* 35, 3 (July 1987), p.413.

14. Born in Trieste to a German-Slovene family, this was the official spelling of his name. Many variants (e.g. Globotschnigg) occur in the literature. Himmler called him 'Globus'.

15. *Hamburger Anzeiger,* 27 March 1940.

16. See the discussion by Bogdan Musial in 'The Origins of "Operation Reinhard": The Decision-Making Process for the Mass Murder of the Jews in the *Generalgouvernement', Yad Vashem Studies* XXVIII (2000). The phrase is taken from Hitler's table talk on 17 October, shortly after the approval by Himmler of Globocnik's plans.

17. *Oberösterreichischer Nachrichten,* 26 April 1946. The author, Simon Wiesenthal, then a young assistant to a US war crimes unit, thought the visit took place in January 1942, but he was describing a preliminary inspection before any building work had been initiated. Wiesenthal was rebuked for making outlandish claims. He took his information from a pamphlet released by the Polish government-in-exile in London.

8

A Deadly Enemy

Provoked by an international outcry about introducing the Star of David and by unhelpful signs of lingering sympathy in Germany towards the Jews, Goebbels composed a short, unsigned commentary setting the stage for future developments. He referred his readers to the latest manifestation of 'sadistic criminality' of Jewry (a German edition of Kaufman's book had just been published on his orders) and to the persistence of hidden Jewish influence. Marking of the Jews had set off a 'lying agitation' around the world, making a mockery of allegations about their mistreatment. But it had woken the German people up, convincing them that the Jewish question must be solved 'without sentimentality'. The whole country 'welcomes every step leading to a real clarification, trusting its leadership will take all necessary further measures at the right time'.[1]

Some Jewish community leaders had been told that deportations were to resume, yet there was no public announcement. The police in Berlin and other cities as well as in the Rhineland were notified only at a late point. Their sudden raids were designed to stun into submission those selected for departure. Families were informed by letter at very short notice, sometimes only a couple of hours beforehand. They were allowed hand luggage, but could not take any belongings or furniture. Ration cards were withdrawn. There were instances of people being coerced into signing statements renouncing their personal property, pensions and other income. Each deportee was charged a fee, so that their removal was self-financing. Suicides occurred. Once a family had left, their home was locked up and under police escort they were marched to a nearby synagogue for the night, or to the local railway station, where they were put on passenger coaches or, failing that, goods carriages, up to a thousand occupants per train. Police spokesmen backed up what they were doing by citing the need for ejecting 'antisocial elements' and owners of 'catastrophe apartments'.[2] A majority of the evacuees were between 50 and 80 years old. Most were going to the ghetto in Lodz (as a result of Eichmann's horse trading), prior to being assigned to forced labour battalions draining the Rokitno marshes near Pinsk, in Ukraine, though the Ministry of Labour had not, as yet, made provision for such an aged workforce. Some were to go on to Riga and Minsk.

In spite of a publicity ban, many Germans realised that a Jewish exodus was under way. Foreign correspondents were also able, often fairly accurately, to find out and directly observe a great deal. The 'abduction' of '20,000' Jews, organised 'by the Gestapo leader Eichmann'[3], was said to be part of a very much larger scheme for removing '200,000' of the Jews of Germany and the Protectorate, to be completed by the turn of the year, leaving only a hardcore of a little under 50,000 younger, economically active Jews. All the aspects of the scheme were not firmly decided, reports suggested, and much depended on the railways. The anomaly of expecting elderly Jews to carry out heavy manual work in the middle of winter bore the stamp – to one London paper – of premeditated mass murder.[4]

Social Demokraten secured another scoop, carrying a story about the closing down without notice of the Jewish Emigration Office in central Berlin.[5] The closure was related to a confidential directive issued by Himmler, purportedly with Hitler's accord, imposing a complete stoppage with 'immediate effect' on any more emigration from Germany and German-controlled Europe. 'Special' (wealthy) individuals might still buy their way out, Himmler allowed. Otherwise the prohibition was absolute, even in the case of small numbers of emigrants such as Spanish Jews living in France who might be transferred to Morocco, as Heydrich explained to the Foreign Office in reply to a Spanish government proposal. Heydrich's extended commission in July specified furthering emigration *and* evacuation. Restrictions on emigrating had been gradually tightened up in recent months. It suited the regime, however, to put the blame on new, quota-based US visa regulations and the closure of many foreign consulates. In slamming the door shut at the very moment when deportations were restarting, the *Reichsführer* was confirming a new policy direction, as well as trapping his prey.

Should Himmler's ban be taken as a foolproof indicator that removal amounted to a death sentence, as one group of scholars maintains? The reasoning seems sensible. So long as the object was to expel the Jews from German soil regardless of whether they lived or not, emigration and evacuation were equally good options for attaining the same end. Provided expulsion was furthered, the means employed were a matter of indifference. Once annihilation became the intended aim, only evacuation coupled with an end to emigration would serve the paramount purpose of catching every last victim. The embryonic efforts to devise local 'solutions', about which Eichmann was still investigating, were supported by propaganda portraying

Jewry as a 'deadly enemy', dangerous if it was left in place to demoralise and subvert but equally malignant if German Jews transported eastwards were able to mix with other Jewish communities and spread their 'noxious' attitudes. Decimation was already an accepted objective. If it was the Jewish 'death wish' to annihilate 80 million German men and women, this could easily be turned upon its creators. But if Hitler had – by this point – issued an unrestricted destruction order, then Himmler's difficulties with the authorities in Lodz are (as Broszat said long ago) 'hardly explicable'.⁶

Events in France were instructive. Following the assassination of two German officers, the German commander in Paris threatened to execute 100 'Communist', 'terrorist' and other hostages unless the culprits were caught. Roosevelt and Churchill publicly expressed their horror at the new 'depths of frightfulness' to which the Nazis were stooping, in France and in other parts of Western Europe but 'above all behind the German fronts in Russia'.⁷ Both committed themselves to stating that those ordering and executing these 'butcheries' would have to answer for their actions. The Nazis, it was observed, had a long history of holding particular populations collectively responsible – currently exemplified by the large-scale arrest and expulsion of Jews in Germany and the Protectorate. Stung by the Allied reaction, Hitler let loose with an outburst while dining with Himmler and Heydrich on the evening of 25 October:

> From the rostrum of the Reichstag I prophesied to Jewry that, in the event of war's proving inevitable, the Jew would disappear from Europe. That race of criminals has on its conscience the two million dead of the First World War, and now already hundreds of thousands more. Let nobody tell me that all the same we can't park them in the marshy parts of Russia! Who's worrying about our troops? It's not a bad idea, by the way, that public rumour attributes to us a plan to exterminate the Jews. Terror is a salutary thing.⁸

Adding fuel to the fire, Goebbels choreographed a press and radio onslaught, tying it to an antisemitic letter published by Antonescu, the Rumanian dictator. Requoting Hitler's 1939 January speech and praising his prophetic gifts, readers were given a reminder of how he had, long before the war began, warned with 'sufficient distinctiveness' what would happen if the Jews were to beget another world war. Time and again Roosevelt by his lust for conflict had ignored or underestimated the earnestness of his adversary. The Jews had incurred 'blood guilt' for which they must atone. That was why they were digging their own graves. It was a just retribution and would be carried out 'to the letter'. Despite the 'disgusting spectacle' of a worldwide clamour, transferring Germany's Jews to certain ghetto areas in the east – 'a necessary security measure' – was as nothing compared with what international Jewry was intending for the Germans. Nonetheless, 'the end has come'.[9]

This blanket coverage served as a preamble to Hitler's annual speech in Munich commemorating the anniversary of the Beer Hall putsch of 1923. Winter had arrived early on the Russian front, he explained, and although German tank units had not managed to encircle Moscow, the Soviet military machine was 'shattered'. Even if the war were to go on for longer, into 1942, German troops would still be victorious. It was a continuation of the same struggle against 'the international Jew' that had been going on since the Great War. Jewish interests had set the world on fire a second time and then spread the flames, glorying in the spillage of blood. This time, he maintained, Germany would hold on to what it was swindled out of in 1918. 'Blockheads' had the deluded idea that they could once again kindle a revolution in Germany. The home front was, however, holding together. Most of the potential miscreants had long since gone abroad to England, America and Canada. Of the few who were left, he had put them where he could see them, watching and waiting. But if they thought they could resist, or if those under German occupation elsewhere resorted to more terrorist acts, he was ready to strike 'like lightning'.

Notes

1. *Berliner Börsen-Zeitung*, 28 September 1941.
2. *The Washington Post*, 28 October 1941. 'Catastrophe apartments' were those being commandeered to accommodate bombed-out German citizens.
3. *The Chicago Sentinel*, 23 October 1941.
4. *Die Zeitung* (London), 21, 24 and 25 October 1941.
5. *Social Demokraten*, 22 October 1941.
6. M. Broszat, 'Hitler und die Genesis der "Endlösung" – Aus Anlass der Thesen von David Irving', in *Vierteljahrshefte für Zeitgeschichte*, 25, 4 (October 1977), p.751.
7. *The Times*, 27 October 1941, reporting on statements released on 25 October.
8. H. Trevor-Roper (ed.), *Hitler's Table Talk* (London: Weidenfeld and Nicolson, 1953), entry dated 25 October 1941. The entry begins with this comment, but it was evidently made in mid-conversation. The 'marshy parts' refers to Rokitno.
9. See (among many others) *Völkischer Beobachter*, 27 October 1941; *Deutsche Allgemeine Zeitung*, 27 October 1941; *Wiener Kronen-Zeitung*, 27 October 1941; *Hamburger Anzeiger*, 27 October 1941; *Berliner Börsen-Zeitung*, 28 October 1941.

9

The Birthday Present

Hitler's Beer Hall denunciation of 'almighty Jewry' for its culpability in causing the war and thwarting German supremacy reflected his realisation that Barbarossa was miscarrying. Resting at Berchtesgaden, he lashed out at 'Roosevelt and his Jews', plaintively asking why the outside world could not 'mind its own business'.[1] The attack on Moscow might still succeed, and yet, as he admitted to his advisers, the Soviets would fight on and neither side was in a position to knock out the other.[2] The upshot was a determination to impose Germany's new European order with even greater ruthlessness, carrying on a struggle with the Jewish race 'that must be seen through to the end and will be seen through to the end'.[3]

Making Germany safe took precedence. The early indications were that the evacuation process was not progressing as briskly as intended. In the three weeks since the first convoys had departed, the full allocation of 20,000 had been relocated to Lodz. More were scheduled to travel up to the *Ostland*, but there were numerous delays and difficulties. In addition to the scarcity of rolling stock, many employers claimed exemptions for those Jews that were part of their own labour force, claiming that replacement workers from the Balkans were unsatisfactory.[4] Half-Jews and those in mixed marriages were also unaffected. The incomplete emptying of cities aggravated the adverse public reaction. In his diary, Goebbels accused 'senior Reich officials' of managing to 'sabotage' the operation.[5]

An American journalist learned that Himmler and Bormann were 'raising Cain', frustrated in their efforts to meet Hitler's end-of-year deadline.[6] In reply to speeches by Roosevelt and the growing bulk of US military *matériel* being supplied to the Soviet Union, Berlin was rumoured to be revising and reinvigorating the deportation programme, fixing a new date of 1 April 1942 for establishing an 'entirely *judenrein*' Germany in time for Hitler's 53rd birthday.[7] The Swiss *Journal de Genève*, citing reputable sources, explained that the expulsions, already 'on a grand scale', were likely to involve a further 20,000 a month, adding that 'though the final plans of the government are not yet known', the Reich Jews were going to Poland where they would participate in important public works for the German war economy.[8]

Goebbels was particularly insistent on forcing the pace, if the memoirs of Felix Kersten, Himmler's doctor and *confidant*, are trustworthy.[9] 'Whether we like it or not', Goebbels phrased it in his weekly article in *Das Reich*, Germany – tethered to a 'hard and unrelenting war' – was being 'driven' to decisions which, 'had the enemy been more yielding', might 'mistakenly' have been shirked. 'We cannot put off anything until tomorrow'.[10] These observations tell us three things. Big decisions were, in his view, pending. Secondly, senior figures were at odds about what should be done. Thirdly, Goebbels wanted the boldest of courses which the 'hard, bitter struggle' waged by the Allies was making essential. With the US Congress revising the Neutrality Act on 13 November to enable American merchant ships to arm themselves and to enter European waters, he used his column the following week to deliver a blistering indictment of Jewish malevolence, stating that Hitler's far-seeing prophecy was being fulfilled and that the Jews were 'perishing' in conformity with their own retaliatory law of 'an eye for an eye and a tooth for a tooth'. Openly referring to the ongoing deportations, he said that removing the Jews was a national duty, a 'hygienic' step that would benefit the unity of the state. They, the Jews in Germany, had 'secret channels' for communicating with Germany's enemies, demonstrated by the fact that every measure that had had to be taken against them was published in the English and American press the very next day. He reeled off a list of ten pithy commandments. All Jews were alike, whether they were living in a ghetto in Poland, swanning around Berlin or banging the drum for war in New York. All were to blame for each German soldier that lost his life. Because of this shared attachment, they did not deserve to be treated decently. Too many Germans were too soft-hearted. Those aiding the Jews were aiding the enemy.[11]

It was a vicious piece, and a revealing one. Eight days later, Gonzalo Montt Rivas, the Chilean consul in Prague (Heydrich's base for the past two months), reported in a despatch to his government that the Jewish problem was being 'partially solved' in the Protectorate by sending some Jews to Poland and others to Theresienstadt. A German victory in the war would leave Europe 'free of Semites', with those 'who escape with their lives' likely to end up in Siberia. Significantly he added that 'in proportion to the USA increasing its attacks on the Reich, Germany will expedite the destruction of Semitism, as she accuses international Judaism of all the calamities that have befallen the world'.[12]

Deportation was one of those matters of, in Goebbels's words, 'decision'. At Hitler's instigation[13], Heydrich decided to bring together all of the main ministries to try to agree on a common approach and eliminate many of the obstacles. Eichmann, just promoted to the rank of *Obersturmbannführer* in recognition of his 'distinguished' service record and responsibility for the evacuation of Jewry, began putting together a briefing paper for Heydrich in mid-November, attaching to it a statistical breakdown of the Jewish population in the each of the countries of Europe. Invitations were then sent out for a meeting to be held at the headquarters of the International Criminal Police Commission in Wannsee on 9 December, the 'extraordinary importance' of the issue requiring an 'identical approach', especially in the light of the deportations from Greater Germany and the Protectorate that had been going on since mid-October.[14] Hitler's 'wish' must be enforced. Himmler had been laying down the law with Wilhelm Stuckart, the State Secretary in the Interior Ministry, instructing him that 'Jewish questions belong to me'. To reinforce his own standing, Heydrich included a photocopy of his *ermächtigung*, an empowerment that few can have already known about. It is of note that several of those who were sent an invitation were unsure about what exactly was to be discussed. The clearing of Jews from Germany, Hitler's present, was without doubt the principal object in mind. But Heydrich's invite pointed to 'a total solution of the Jewish question in Europe', which explains why a representative from the Foreign Office was also asked to attend.

Two colleagues had been uncooperative. Hans Frank's obstinacy was unchanged. By blocking any more German Jews from entering his territory, he was underlining his unwillingness to relinquish control of Jewish policy in the *General Gouvernement*. He understood that opinion was shifting, however. If, as he taunted them on the radio, the Jews were moved a few thousand kilometres eastwards, what of it? The able-bodied could be organised into road-building gangs. As for the remainder, 'we must provide suitable arrangements'. How much Frank knew about Globocnik's initiatives that were taking place under his nose is uncertain. But after consulting with Friedrich-Wilhelm Krüger, the Higher SS and Police official in the *General Gouvernement*, Heydrich extended an invitation to Frank's deputy, Josef Bühler.

The dispute with Rosenberg's *Ostministerium* had also not died down. Lohse was still refusing to accept any transports. The ghetto in Riga was far too congested, he insisted. The camp at Salaspils was uncompleted. The risk to security presented by so many cultured German Jews, as the senior army commander said, made their arrival 'quite impossible'. At the last moment

Lohse attempted to have them sent elsewhere. Himmler overcame the impasse by appointing a new Higher SS and Police leader for North Russia and the *Ostland*, Friedrich Jeckeln, the executor of the first truly mass killing – of 33,000 Jews – in Kiev at the end of September. Jeckeln was told in the strongest terms to 'liquidate' the Riga ghetto and to make it crystal clear to Lohse that it was a Himmler and therefore a Hitler order which must be carried out in spite of Lohse's reservations. Jeckeln, in his confession in 1946, said the point was to empty the ghetto and free the space for the arrivals from Germany.

Lohse, after speaking with Jeckeln, took it up with Rosenberg, who agreed to see Hitler on his behalf. While waiting for a response, Lohse released new instructions reiterating his opposition to shootings occurring without his knowledge – though he was not opposed to the 'cleansing' of the *Ostland* as such (as was shown by the Wetzel episode) – and asking if there was a general 'liquidation' decree which he had somehow missed. But where Frank was obdurate, Rosenberg was far more timid with Hitler, with whom he had an interview on 14 November, suffering a flat 'rebuff'.[15] In an uneasy agreement of sorts with Himmler, Rosenberg recognised that the handling of the Jews was 'essentially a police matter', while claiming a right to 'civil oversight'.[16] At a press conference to launch the work of his fledgling ministry, he remarked that there were some 6 million Jews 'in the east' who were part of a larger problem which could only be solved by the 'biological eradication' of the whole of European Jewry, either by forcing them over the Urals or in some other way. He qualified this, however, by referring to the economic needs of wartime. Lohse soon caved in, agreeing to attend a shooting 'action' to gain his 'own impression'.

What was intended is very much a moot point. Those transported to Minsk were kept alive. Because the Riga camp in Salaspils was unfinished, others ended up in Kovno, Lithuania's second city, where they were all executed by the local security police. On 30 November Lohse was present when the first Jews to reach Riga – a convoy from Berlin – were 'disposed of' too, probably because the ghetto was not yet sufficiently reduced. In an urgent phone call, Heydrich had tried to prevent the shooting but was too late. Himmler followed this up by sending a cable to Jeckeln, telling him off for flouting the guidelines. That Jews with war decorations had inadvertently been among the deportees may have been the key concern. The salient aspect is that treatment varied so much, largely due to the disorganised race against time.

Urging an 'energetic' approach to clear the *Altreich* and the Protectorate, Hitler was already looking ahead. As he told one guest, the Grand Mufti of

Jerusalem, Germany had declared 'an uncompromising war on the Jews', committing itself to the 'obliteration' of the last vestiges of Jewish-communist European hegemony. He said he would challenge European nations one-by-one to settle the Jewish issue.[17] The Mufti, who is thought to have met Himmler and Eichmann during the same visit, was also assured that when the time came Germany would terminate the Jewish homeland in Palestine. At a two-day convening in Berlin of the members of the Anti-Komintern Pact, Hitler, Himmler and Goering each put forward the case for developing their alliance against Bolshevism into an economic and political *bloc*. Hitler, styled 'the saviour of Europe' because he had pre-empted a Soviet invasion, pointed out how Germany had always carried the 'blood burden' in order to free its neighbours from ideological disruption and racial contamination.[18] The twelve other nations were encouraged to co-ordinate their domestic security policies, especially regarding anti-Jewish legislation, starting with the adoption of the Yellow Star marking for Jews. Germany's attitude was 'irrevocable' – the Jews were to quit the continent once fighting had ceased. In effect the Pact's members were being given an ultimatum, as Goering told the Danish Foreign Minister, that if they did not 'rapidly' decide by themselves then Germany would do it for them. To those countries who thought the British, the Americans and the Soviets were growing in strength, Ribbentrop dismissed any prospect of Churchill's subterfuges succeeding. 'The tank and the dive-bomber preclude the possibility of revolt in disarmed territory.'[19] By creating a common front they were ensuring that this would be 'the last ever Jewish war'.[20]

In a wide-ranging lecture at the German Academy before an audience of high-ranking officials, army officers and cultural leaders, Goebbels, while expressing a favourable view of the military prospects, spoke about a number of problems in need, he said, of urgent attention. Definitively solving the Jewish problem was 'one of the first and most important tasks of the coming period'. In a hard-headed 'overview' of the issue, he referred once again to the *Führer*'s prophecy, which 'we are living through the fulfilment of'. The Jews 'wanted their war and now they have it', which was why they were being subjected to a 'gradual', wholly justifiable 'process of extermination' – 'gradual' implying the dying out of Jewry by a combination of expulsion, lack of food, debilitating ill health and, in the east, the culling of the 'surplus' and the rebellious. Sticking to generalities, he was emphatic that they were heading in a direction from which there could be no pulling back. With his eye on the Wannsee meeting in a few days' time, some, he admonished, apt to use 'sentimental' Jew-friendly arguments, were 'lagging behind'. The responsibility of the national leadership was to address the Jewish question 'by whatever appropriate means'. Europe, not just Germany, had laboured under Jewish domination. The ending of that domination would signal the birth of a new Europe.[21]

Notes

1. P. Huss, *The Foe We Face* (Garden City, NY: Doubleday, Doran and Co, 1942), Chapter 12 ('An interview with Hitler', in the first few days of November 1941).
2. K. Reinhardt, 'Moscow 1941 – the Turning-Point" in J. Erickson and D. Dilks (eds), *Barbarossa: the Axis and the Allies* (Edinburgh: Edinburgh University Press, 1994), p.219-220.
3. *Völkischer Beobachter*, 12 November 1941.
4. The Jewish Telegraphic Agency news bulletin, 5 November 1941.
5. E. Fröhlich (ed.), *Die Tagebücher von Joseph Goebbels*, II, 2 (Munich: K.G. Saur, 1996), entry dated 28 October 1941.
6. Huss, *The Foe We Face*, p.252.
7. *The Daily Mirror*, 8 November 1941. See also Joseph Grigg's account in *The New York World-Telegram* of 1 June 1942. Accessed on 14 February 2021 from: http://haolusa.org/index.php?en/main-650-whoknew.ssi). Grigg, a US foreign correspondent in Germany, was interned for five months after Pearl Harbor before being released.
8. *Le Journal de Genève*, 7 November 1941.
9. F. Kersten, *The Kersten Memoirs 1940-1945* (London: Hutchinson, 1956), especially pp.119-21 and 160-4. Kersten learnt from Himmler on 11 November that 'the destruction of the Jews is being planned', encouraged by Goebbels and Bormann. Edouard Husson (*Heydrich et la Solution Finale* (Paris: Perrin, 2008)) thinks this dating is of vital importance. Himmler's own desk diary does not indicate an appointment with Kersten on or around that time (for a discussion see F. Brayard, 'Shoah: l'intuition et la preuve' in *La Vie des Idées* (12 February 2009). Accessed on 14 February 2021 from: http://www.laviedesidees.fr/Shoah-l-intuition-et-la-preuve.html). Kersten's book was printed in five different versions between 1947 and 1956 and did not seem to have been based on written records, prompting some critics to allege that he embellished his recollections. One critic calls him a 'fraud'.
10. *Das Reich*, 9 November 1941.
11. *Das Reich*, 16 November 1941. Goebbels had also spotted comments by Churchill 'taking the side of the Jews' in his Mansion House speech of 10 November. Churchill suggested that Communists and Jews executed by the Nazis ought to be regarded 'as if they were brave soldiers who died for their country on the field of battle' (*The Manchester Guardian*, 11 November 1941).
12. A copy of the despatch became available in the US National Archives in 2001. See R. Breitman's 'What Chilean diplomats learned about the Holocaust' of 20 June 2001. Accessed on 14 February 2021 from: https://www.archives.gov/iwg/research-papers/breitman-chilean-diplomats.html.
13. Eichmann told this to the journalist, Willem Sassen, who interviewed him over several months in 1956 and 1957 – 'It was Hitler himself – neither Heydrich nor Himmler,

they were not the initiators. No, of this I am sure ...'. Accessed on 14 February 2021 from: https://nizkor.com/ftp.cgi/people/e/ftp.cgi?people/e//eichmann.adolf/transcripts/Sessions/Session-075-03).

14. N. Kampe, 'Besprechung über der Judenfrage – Das Protokoll der Wannsee-Konferenz am 20 Januar 1942'. Accessed on 14 February 2021 from: https://www.fritz-bauer institu.de/fileadmin/editorial/publikationen/einsicht/einsicht-07.pdf, pp.28-29. On 4 December the venue was switched (possibly the Interpol address was used in error in the first letters of invitation) to another, larger villa on the main part of Lake Wannsee.

15. See the *zeugenschrift* of Otto Bräutigam in the archive of the Institut für Zeitgeschichte in Munich (ZS-400/3-37 and 38). Accessed on 14 February 2021 from http://www.ifz-muenchen.de/archiv/zs/zs-0400_3.pdf.

16. J. Matthäus and F. Bajohr (eds), *The Political Diary of Alfred Rosenberg* (Lanham, MD: Rowman & Littlefield, 2015), p.458.

17. See G. Fleming, *Hitler and the Final Solution* (Berkeley, CA: University of California Press, 1984), Chapter 11.

18. See Hitler's talk with the Finnish Foreign Minister on 27 November 1941, in *Akten zur Deutschen Auswärtigen Politik – 1918-1945*, D, XIII, 2 (Göttingen: Vandenhoeck & Ruprecht, 1970).

19. *The Manchester Guardian*, 27 November 1941.

20. *Der Südostdeutsche Tageszeitung*, 30 November 1941.

21. *Völkischer Beobachter*, 3 December 1941. A fuller version of the text is in J. Herf, *The Jewish Enemy – Nazi Propaganda during World War II and the Holocaust* (Cambridge, MA: Harvard University Press, 2006), pp.124-7. Herf points out that, apart from quoting Hitler, Goebbels's own explicit reference to 'extermination' was omitted in the press reports of the lecture.

10

Wendepunkt

Twenty-four hours before Heydrich's Wannsee guests were due to assemble, they found out from a phone call that owing to 'suddenly announced events' the meeting was postponed indefinitely. These events dramatically transformed the war. They also, by extension, had a profound impact on the subject matter of Wannsee.

In the first few days of December, Hitler had flown down to the southern sector of the Russian front in a highly agitated state. His troops were ready to drop and, ill-equipped and exposed to the elements, were in grave danger. Field Marshal von Rundstedt, in command of Army Group South, wanted to disengage and pull back to more easily defendable positions and had withdrawn from the city of Rostov, the army's first major reverse of the campaign. Hitler replaced von Rundstedt with General von Reichenau, but von Reichenau soon persuaded Hitler of the soundness of von Rundstedt's opinion. The situation was little better in the central part of the front, the troops halted before Moscow in freezing temperatures and similarly exhausted. Returning to Rastenberg in the midst of this crisis, news came through of a Japanese air strike on the American naval base at Pearl Harbor.

Though it took Hitler two days to make it clear, a German declaration of war on the United States was very much a foregone conclusion. Germany and Italy were bound by the terms of the Tripartite Pact to 'assist' Japan if it was attacked by another non-European power, but Ribbentrop had also assured the Japanese that they would 'of course' take Japan's side in any conflict with the US. The German general staff had been praying for the Japanese to intervene in the Soviet Far East, threatening Siberia. Even so, Japan's assault on Pearl Harbor and targets in South-East Asia had many compensating advantages. American naval strength had suffered a massive hit. The US would have to shift resources from the Atlantic to the Pacific, weakening the convoy supply route to Britain which German U-Boats could freely attack. Britain too would be distracted by its endangered Asian possessions. With Japan as a military partner, a jubilant Hitler felt that the global balance of forces was tilting in his favour.

After arriving back in Berlin, he addressed a special session of the Reichstag, anxious to prove he still held the initiative. He accused the United States, and the Jews around Roosevelt 'with their Old Testament vindictiveness', of a long history of hostility towards National Socialist Germany, launching into a detailed recital of successive incitements and provocations, their increasingly overt belligerence demonstrating the desire to bring about a second slaughter in Europe. The Neutrality Act, designed to hold a President in check, was cynically circumvented. Anglo-Saxon plutocrats and Jewish Bolsheviks were now fully aligned, just as expected. For his part, he had been trying to spare the world from another conflagration. But the Americans were thirsting for world conquest. He was left with no other choice but to acknowledge that the two countries were, had in fact for some time been, in an open state of war. America would be wholly at fault for what was to follow, 'to the ultimate consequence'.[1] Faced by this new reality, the demands made on the German nation would be even more exacting. He recognised there had been heavy and mounting casualties (160,000 dead) in the east but this loss was justified if Germany was to succeed in establishing its right to life. 'History does not repeat itself.' Any 'internal doubts' were unacceptable. Nothing and nobody should be allowed to stand in the way of attaining final victory.

The speech was shot through with personal abuse. Hitler stopped short, however, of directly alluding to his prophecy. He brought it up instead on the following day, 12 December, in a gathering in his private quarters in the Chancellery of 50 of the party's Gauleiters and apparatchiks – a meeting which only came to light with the release of the complete run of the diaries of Goebbels in 1996.[2] In a lengthy assessment of the way the war would develop now that it had taken on a global character, Hitler spoke plainly about what he had foretold, paraphrased by Goebbels in a few crisp sentences. The world war which the Jews had been working for had at long last broken out. They had engineered it and they would be the ones to pay the penalty. He had warned them of this on many occasions. His warnings were not just hot air. He had meant every word. The Jews must reap what they had sown. Germany was sacrificing its best people. The Jews too would lose their lives. The moment had come to 'wipe the table clean'.[3]

What did he want to convey and how did it fit in with the aim of quickening the deportation of Germany's Jews?

In an eye-catching essay, Christian Gerlach has claimed that Hitler's comments represent the 'missing piece' in the historical jigsaw puzzle about when and why Hitler had ordered that the Jews of Europe should be put to death.[4] His argument was cogently expressed. Hitler's referencing of his prophecy had never before been so 'unequivocal' and 'matter of fact'. It was a world war now because the 'other world' – America – was joining in. Henceforth the Jews of Germany lost any diplomatic value as helpless hostages. The prophecy, since Hitler was bound to be opposed by the other major powers, was 'self-fulfilling'. The suggestions of an authorisation in high summer (with the expansion of shooting to encompass all Soviet Jews) or autumn (coinciding with the restarting of deportation) were erroneous. Here, with the whole world at war again, was the elusive *Führerbefehl*, a basic ordering of an annihilation policy as a point of principle, leaving it up to Himmler and Heydrich to work out the technicalities and tempo. Gerlach went further. He took into account the haphazard and arbitrary treatment of the first trainloads of expelled German Jews in October and November, which suggested to him that to begin with there was no certainty about what to do with them. Wannsee was to have been principally concerned with that important but limited issue. The postponement of the conference enabled Heydrich and others to adjust to the wholly new context created by Hitler concerning the very much larger task of removing *and eliminating* German, eastern and in time all the Jews – a clean sweep – across the entire European continent. Notes of what Hans Frank relayed in mid-December to his cabinet members in Krakow about his recent talks in Berlin started to make sense. The Jews, as Hitler had once said, must be finished off. There was to be a major conference to discuss this 'gigantic' task. The 2.5 million Jews of the *General Gouvernement* were also under consideration. 'We cannot shoot these' and 'we cannot poison them' but he, Frank, was confident of finding a way 'somehow' to successfully ensure that they 'disappear'.[5]

Gerlach's article caused a great stir, largely, it must be said, because of the objections of those who were unpersuaded.[6] Hitler's speech to the Gauleiters was 'routine', one of his usual rants, and was 'nothing special', Mommsen thought. Some doubted whether Hitler would have unveiled such a significant decision, if that was what it was, before such a modest audience. Gerlach had 'over-interpreted' the evidence, which could not support the weight he was attaching to it. Hitler was simply restating something that had already been decided. Or (alternatively) it was at most a gradual hardening of position which – incidentally – was blatantly contrived given that it was he himself who, however he tried to dress it up differently, had declared war on the US.

Gerlach's misconstruing of two individual items of some pertinence did not help his case. Both had to do with the 'sudden flurry' of activity in the days after the Gauleiter meeting. The first is a notation in Himmler's desk diary for 18 December (Gerlach was a member of the team editing Himmler's diaries in the 1990s), apparently highlighting the points he intended to bring up in conversation that day with Hitler. Next to '*Judenfrage*', the Jewish question, had been added – in tinier handwriting – the words 'to be exterminated as partisans'.[7] Gerlach, agreeing that it was tricky to interpret, took this to mean Hitler meant the 'Final Solution' of the *Judenfrage* as a whole, confirming what he had said in the Reich Chancellery. It was of a piece, as such, with the recognition that the wider war required dealing definitively with the Jews. Gerlach's interpretation seemed, for many, to be a rather strained reading of a short scribble.[8] Surely, it was conjectured, the 'partisan' term was easily traceable to the conference the previous July, at which Hitler urged a tough response to partisan warfare by the Soviets, and could have little relevance to western Europe, where opposition to German rule tended to be described as 'terroristic'.[9]

The second item is a letter of the same date from the *Ostministerium*, replying after some weeks to Lohse's request in mid-November for guidance. Lohse had learned by this stage of the brush-off Rosenberg was given by Hitler. It is likely that Lohse was present with the other Gauleiters when Hitler addressed them. He cannot have been left in any doubt that he should cease and desist from impeding any further 'actions'. Bräutigam was now informing him that, following 'oral discussions' about the Jewish question, 'economic factors' (i.e. retaining valuable Jewish labour) were not to be taken into consideration. Bräutigam provided additional clarification in his autobiography. Jewish tailors and shoemakers in White Russia, adjoining the *Ostland*, were crucial in the provisioning of uniforms for the German army and his colleagues were convinced eradicating them would be counter-productive. Much to their surprise, Hitler dogmatically insisted that the Jewish problem took precedence over all other issues and that economic considerations should play no part; he could only solve matters by eliminating hostile elements immediately behind the frontline, where, mixed up with the general fighting, police operations would be less apparent.[10] Like the note in Himmler's diary, the document, on the face of it, dealt only with the activities of the *Einsatzgruppen*. Gerlach asserts that Bräutigam was not privy to the bigger picture, which is possible but unprovable.

In his favour, however, Gerlach's account fully measures up to the colossal scale of the changes to the wartime balance of force in December 1941 and to Hitler's belief, attested to by Frank, that winning the war would only partly be a success if Germany lost its finest soldiers and the Jews of

Europe survived. The blunt simplicity of Goebbels's summary is characteristically hard-nosed. Lammers conceded that some of Hitler's weightiest decisions were communicated only to the leadership *corps* of the Gauleiters. It is also worth recalling Hitler saying in September that he was holding back with a total expulsion order of the Jews until the US was firmly in the war. Roosevelt had been steadily adopting a warlike posture without jumping in with both feet, and Hitler had ratcheted up his anti-Jewish responses in an effort to dissuade and deter. To all intents and purposes, however, the two countries were already warring with each other. From this point forward, Hitler's objective was not deterrence but vengeance. A declaration of war on America was his way of making 'the real world conform to his vision of the world'[11], validating what he intended to do next.[12]

By the time Hitler was able to turn his full attention back to the battleground in Russia, things had deteriorated. The Red Army had made several forward thrusts, especially to relieve Moscow. German forces were at the end of their strength, Fritz Halder (head of the Army High Command) gloomily recorded in his diary, and there was a very real fear that they could in places be put to flight, abandoning vital heavy equipment in a headlong retreat.[13] Hitler's reaction was to assume direct personal control, formally appointing himself as Supreme Commander. The army, he insisted, was to go over to a defensive footing, digging in and holding firm. In a statement to the troops on 19 December, he explained why he had accepted the 'calling'. The war, sought by Jewish-capitalist interests, had reached a critical turning-point (*wendepunkt*) of 'worldwide' import. Their Japanese comrades were wreaking havoc on British and American interests in East Asia. At the same time the Wehrmacht on the eastern front, displaying its resilience in confronting 'the most dangerous enemy of all time', had taken up a fixed position, protecting the continent of Europe until the spring, when they could resume the offensive. In heralding a 'total' war – for which it was not really prepared, either militarily or economically – he called for front and home to unite in one common effort.[14]

Over the next couple of weeks, though many German divisions were obliged to pull back, in some places eventually by as much as 200 kilometres, the position was stabilised. It is generally agreed that Hitler's intervention averted a Napoleonic disaster. Premonitions of defeat and death heightened his awareness of the elemental ends of the conflict. He was troubled by the enormous loss of German blood, even though in the longer run it would ensure 'the same criminals' would not be able to go on setting off a new war every few decades. In the past the Jews had been able to get away with it. He would see to it that they paid up in full. The time for conscience was over. If the problem was left for someone else to tackle later, it would be devastatingly difficult. They *had* to be shoved off to the east. What happened to them there could be of no further concern, except to say they had wished it upon themselves.[15] New punishments for Poles and Jews challenging German authority in the *Ostgebiet* were brought in.[16] Associated reports were circulating to the effect that Jews in other countries, most notably France, were also to be rounded up and deported to the same region.[17]

The parallels with 1918 were, in Hitler's obsessive thinking, stark. Germany had, out of necessity, been forced into striking first. He had had to risk everything, making a superhuman effort to overthrow the Soviet state. Cheated of a swift victory, after one final push – akin to Ludendorff's ill-fated venture in early 1918 – he was now facing a formidable enemy. This time, however, though many of his senior army officers were losing heart, he was not going to permit the German military to disintegrate. By fusing political and army authority in his hands, he prevented any shuffling off of responsibility by the generals. The humiliation of the *Weltkrieg* was cancelled out. Germany was not near breaking point. The Winter Clothing Relief campaign (providing the poorly provisioned troops with warm clothing that the planners had been told would not be needed) had shown this, dispelling the illusion of the Jews that Germany was about to capitulate yet again. But the menace of rebellions was an ever-present anxiety. Those longing to profit from Germany going under must be dealt with. In so doing the Jewish 'conspiracy' (he said in his New Year statement) would be broken up and eliminated for many generations.

A war on two fronts effectively meant a war on all fronts, against external enemies but also against those many enemies within that Europe was riddled with. In a struggle for self-preservation, nothing was ruled out. A 'remarkable' article credited to *Der Angriff*, Goebbels's own flagship paper, communicated what he took from his talks with Hitler and his own eagerness to scold those German 'traitors', disconcerted by the Nazi persecution of the Jews, who were showing signs of greater pro-Jewish friendliness. Berlin's Jews, as Goebbels was nagging colleagues about, were fraternising more widely than before, courted by Germans worrying about the way the tide was turning. 'If Germany is defeated', Swedish newspapers summarised the paper saying, 'the Nazis will exterminate all Jews in Nazi-occupied countries first. We will not allow the Jews to inherit Germany'.[18]

Notes

1. *Hamburger Anzeiger*, 12 December 1941.
2. The only contemporary report of the meeting, in a story emanating from Stockholm in *The New York Times* of 15 December 1941, was one suggesting that 'at a meeting of all the German Gauleiters (Nazi regional leaders) that Hitler summoned three days ago', they had warned him of the wave of pessimism likely to break out once the public appreciated the seriousness of the failure to capture Moscow and the scale of the retreats. Allied sources judged it to be part of a disinformation campaign to encourage US public opinion to become complacent (see *The Rotarian*, December 1942).
3. E. Fröhlich (ed.), *Die Tagebücher von Joseph Goebbels* (Munich: K.G. Saur, 1996), II, 2, entry dated 13 December 1941.
4. Originally published in German in 1997, Gerlach's essay was republished in an English translation, 'The Wannsee Conference, the Fate of German Jews, and Hitler's Decision in Principle to Exterminate All European Jews', in *The Journal of Modern History*, 70, 4 (December 1998), pp.759-812.
5. *Nazi Conspiracy and Aggression*, IV (Washington, DC: US Government Printing Office, 1946), pp.891-2.
6. *The Times*, 14 January 1998; *The New York Times*, 21 January 1998; *The Observer-Reporter*, 21 January 1998; *Le Monde*, 24 January 1998. See also the critiques by Christopher Browning, in his *Nazi Policy, Jewish Workers and German Killers* (Cambridge: Cambridge University Press, 2000), pp.33-56, and Ian Kershaw, 'Hitler and the Holocaust', in his *Hitler, the Germans and the Final Solution* (New Haven, CT: Yale University Press, 2008), pp.237-81.
7. P. Witte et al (eds), *Der Dienstkalender Heinrich Himmlers 1941/42* (Hamburg: Hans Christians Verlag, 1999), entry dated 18 December 1941.
8. There is an interesting treatment of the semantic nuances of this phrase in Florent Brayard's '"A exterminer en tant que partisans" – sur une note de Himmler', in *Politix*, 2008/2 (no.82), pp.9-37. Accessed on 15 February 2021 from: https://www.cairn.info/revue-politix-2008-2-page-9.htm.
9. J. Stengers, 'Himmler et l'extermination de 30 millions de Slaves', in *Vingtième Siècle*, 71, 1 (2001), footnote 8, p.4.
10. O. Bräutigam, *So hat es sich zugetragen* (Würzburg: Holzner Verlag,1968), p.414.
11. E. Husson, *Heydrich et la Solution Finale* (Paris: Perrin, 2008), p.485.
12. A high-ranking security service defector, speaking to Swiss intelligence in 1944, affirmed that Germany undertook the total liquidation of the Jews of Europe only 'after the US entered the war' and 'on the order of the Fuhrer' (*Le Journal de Genève*, 21-22 April 1979).
13. War Journal of Fritz Halder, VII, entry dated 8 (mistyped 6 in the original) December 1941. Accessed on 15 February from: http://cgsc.contentdm.oclc.org/cdm/singleitem/collection/p4013coll8/id/3974/rec/3.
14. *Der Angriff*, 23 December 1941.
15. See Fröhlich (ed.), *Die Tagebücher von Joseph Goebbels*, entry dated 18 December 1941.
16. *Völkischer Beobachter*, 25-26 December 1941.
17. *The Palestine Post*, 23 December 1941, relying on claims in Stockholm.
18. *The Chicago Sentinel*, 25 December 1941.

11

The Conference

This assertiveness was clearly evident when, in early January, Heydrich set a new date – 20 January – for the State Secretaries to meet in Wannsee. Hitler and Goebbels had spoken with each other about 'totally solving' the Jewish problem. The Reich was known to be preparing to 'rid Europe of its Jews' in a comprehensive resettlement, satisfied that forging a Jewless Europe would contribute to the triumph of German arms. Transports from Germany had continued but, although the possibility of an Anglo-American attempt to immediately open up a second front in western Europe was slight, the SS began to take much greater notice of the so far unmarked Jews in France, Holland and Belgium. Himmler issued a fresh instruction to tighten up the October ban on emigration from the German sphere of influence, concerned that many Dutch and Belgian Jews were avoiding deportation by making their way down to the unoccupied southern half of France, where exit visas were still obtainable.[1] Officials were leant on to do as they were told. Lösener (the Jewish affairs expert in the Interior Ministry), discovering just before Christmas about the shooting of Berlin Jews in Riga, went to his immediate superior, Stuckart, to ask for a transfer. 'Don't you know', Stuckart told him, 'that these things are happening on the highest orders?'[2] In a handwritten note found among Lösener's papers after his death, Stuckart had gone on to say that Germany had Jewry to thank for having to fight the war, which, from the standpoint of world historical necessity, had to be fought with hardness, irrespective of whether or not this or that evacuated Jew was individually at fault.[3]

For Himmler and Heydrich, their dilemma was territorial. All their efforts had been devoted to finding a quick fix, relocating German Jews wherever they could before moving them on again in the near future. Some of these had been disposed of in the meantime. The military deadlock put paid to any hope of sending any of the others off to the far-flung labour camps of the Soviet GULAG. The *General Gouvernement*, Frank's *nebenland*, with its own sizeable number of indigenous Jews – Warsaw alone had over half-a-million, although malnutrition and disease were taking their toll – was effectively out of bounds. Frank knew from his conversations in December that the issue, under Heydrich's leadership, was coming to the boil; he was also dead set on deciding matters for himself. Himmler made an arrangement. Having talked with Eberhard Schöngarth, the Higher SS and Police leader in Krakow, he saw Bühler, due to appear at Wannsee on Frank's behalf, discussing, it is thought, how to ease the population pressure in the region.[4] Along the lines already adopted, 'unproductive' Jews could be relocated 'eastwards', loosely speaking. The presence in Berlin in mid-January of Heinz Auerswald, the administrator of the Warsaw ghetto, is a corroborative detail.[5] By priming Bühler, Himmler was making it possible for the ghettos to begin to be liquidated, creating room for future deportations.

Heydrich greeted his fourteen guests to Am Grossen Wannsee at midday on the same day that a new government was taking office in Prague, his measures to bring the Protectorate to heel (which included six trainloads of deported Czech Jews to Lodz and Minsk) assisting in its 'progressive pacification'.[6] His manner was businesslike. He had, he explained in his opening remarks, been commissioned the previous July by Goering to handle the preparations for 'the Final Solution of the Jewish Question in Europe'. In order to be in a position to report back to Goering – and Hitler[7] – with a 'draft' plan of the organisational, policy and technical prerequisites, it was necessary to organise and 'harmonize' the views of all the relevant central agencies. Irrespective of geographical boundaries, the *Reichsführer* was in 'overall control'. He then gave a review of what had occurred since January 1939, describing the policy of the emigration of Jews from Germany, the drawbacks this involved, and how, given the dangers in wartime, emigration had been superseded with Hitler's 'prior approval' (in September) by the evacuation of Jews to the east. The first wave of these evacuations had already been carried out, and although only temporary, the practical experience gained was of great value for 'the coming Final Solution of the Jewish Question'.

What, in outline, was this 'draft' solution? The Jewish inhabitants of the entirety of the European mainland, German and German-occupied as well as neutral and enemy territory (the list naming England, Ireland, Sweden, Switzerland, Spain, Portugal and the USSR) totalling approximately 11 million people, were to be combed out, country-by-country, firstly in Germany proper and then from western to eastern Europe. Leaving to one side enemy states, Martin Luther, the Foreign Ministry representative, advised that only the Scandinavians were likely to present any great difficulties 'if this problem is dealt with thoroughly'. Under 'suitable leadership', Heydrich resumed, the able-bodied were 'now' going to be transported by-and-by to 'transit ghettos' before being forwarded on to the east, where they would be sorted into large, single-sex working parties (this, as is shown by other documentation, was already happening in some parts of the eastern areas, where Hitler agreed to the use of Jewish labour in road construction[8]). Most, 'without doubt', were likely to perish from 'natural causes'. The remainder, the hardiest, would have to be dealt with 'appropriately' so that they could not form the biological basis for a Jewish 'revival'. As for the elderly (over the age of 65), including war veterans, they were to be confined in ghettos, possibly in Theresienstadt. Several key points, by this stage of Heydrich's summary, were apparent. German Jews – who were to go first – and the rest of Europe's Jews who would follow were to be treated identically. The proposed treatment was attritional and, ultimately, homicidal. They would do away with the Jewish problem by doing away with the Jews. A timetable for implementation of the larger evacuations was not mentioned, but depended, Heydrich accepted, on 'the military situation' and the goodwill of allied regimes.

After this, pursuing his intention to establish the ground rules 'in a legal way', he raised the issue of defining the exact criteria for those who were to be 'affected'. Were Jews of mixed blood or in mixed marriages to be deported? Heydrich said he had received a letter from Lammers, the head of the Reich Chancellery. Puzzled by what the 'Final Solution' entailed, Lammers had been to see Himmler and Hitler (so he later asserted in two slightly different versions).[9] An 'evasive' Hitler had told him he had given Himmler an order to begin evacuating the Jews but that he did not wish to discuss it. Lammers may, in which case, have been notifying Heydrich that the Chancellery was not inclined for the moment to take a position. Lammers's colleague, Kritzinger, did not speak up during the conference. Heydrich proceeded to talk 'theoretically', describing the various inclusions and exceptions that had to be considered, always with a view to weeding out characteristics which were racially 'undesirable'. Stuckart, the senior Interior Ministry civil servant who as noted was well-informed, tried to gain time, suggesting the widespread use of forced sterilisation of half-Jews, which would, he believed, avoid 'endless administrative work'. Since the issue was not settled, Heydrich accepted it needed further examination.[10]

Finally, to reassure Goering's Ministry for the Four-Year Plan, Heydrich added that, consistent with the guidelines he was operating on, Jews employed in war industries could not be evacuated until replacement labour was found.

At this point, towards the end, Bühler made his move. He said he would 'welcome' it if the 'Final Solution' could begin not, as Heydrich had

visualised, from west to east but in the *General Gouvernement*. This would not present such a transport problem (in addition to a number of transit camps, Poland also had a densely developed rail system). Because of the current risk of epidemics there was a strong argument for urgency. Black market activity, too, was rife. In any case, he added, most of the two-and-a-quarter million Jews were incapable of working (*arbeitsunfähig* – the word was underlined in the circulated summary). Recognising that the authority to act was entirely in Heydrich's hands, Bühler pressed him to solve the Jewish question in the *General Gouvernement* 'as quickly as possible'.

'In conclusion', the 'various possible solutions were discussed', with both Bühler and Meyer, the Secretary of State in the Eastern Ministry, taking the view that certain preparatory measures should be begun in 'the territories in question, without alarming the populace'. After an hour-and-a-half, Heydrich brought the meeting to a close with a last nod to his commission from Goering, requesting that all those present would provide him with the necessary co-operation and assistance.

Having expected trouble, Heydrich was surprised by how enthusiastically senior officials fell into line. Meyer, so stubborn in October, was constructive. Stuckart's 'compromise' exceeded all expectations. The obstructionists had not forgotten Goebbels's sharp reprimands, deciding that it was unwise to outwardly oppose a plan that was being sanctioned from on high. Bühler's part was also decisive, ceding control to the SS in return for an early start on emptying Poland of its Jews.

There are many imponderables. Are the 'minutes', if this is an acceptable word to describe them, a full and accurate rendering of who said exactly what?[11] Eichmann is on record admitting his notes were worked on and 'polished' afterwards, making liberal use of several euphemisms. Can there be any truth in the suggestion that the protocol was distorted or falsified? The biggest bone of contention is about the degree of openness with which the ultimate issue – life or death? – was addressed. Peter Longerich has referred to the 'sinister omission' from Heydrich's speech of any mention of the disabled.[12] Bühler's candid comments on this score certainly give the game away, especially in view of attempts in the *General Gouvernement* to hamper Jewish employment.[13] So, it might be held, did Stuckart's proposition which presupposed that half-Jews would prefer sterilisation to deportation. Meyer knew about the use of gas vans; Georg Leibbrandt, his colleague, probably did too. Heinrich Müller (head of the Gestapo) and Eichmann, two of the six members of the SS who attended, kept quiet, while Lange and Schöngarth both had blood on their hands from overseeing the work of the *Einsatzgruppen*. It hardly seems tenable, with so many so embroiled in what was already going on, to imagine that nothing much was decided at Wannsee and that several of the participants were unaware of the full background. The Wannsee transcript, after all, is confirmation 'in black and white' of an objective to at least procure the extinction of Europe's Jews.[14]

The security aim clearly conflicted with the economic one. '*Endsieg*' (final victory) depended on the '*Endlösung*'. Too many Jews were being sheltered. But many of the skilled Jewish artisans in German-occupied Europe were, for now, irreplaceable. Heydrich cannot have been unaware of the critical conference taking place on the same day to consider armament and labour requirements as the war entered a new phase.[15] Could an out-and-out annihilation programme take place under the guise of the redeployment of slave labour?

Hitler, who had initiated the conference, was brought up-to-date by Himmler, the two of them lunching with Lammers on 25 January.[16] His verdict – *his* timetabling – was to press ahead with despatch. 'It must be done quickly.' In the circumstances, 'I'm enormously humane'. If on their journey they 'break down', it could not be helped. They would not go voluntarily, so their 'complete eradication' (*absolut ausrottung*) was the only way. They were no different from Soviet POWs, many of whom were dying in prison camps.[17] What could he do about it? he asked aloud. He had been put in this position. Why had the Jews started the war?

Heydrich had justified evacuating all the Jews of Europe in one go by citing 'the lessons of history'. Hitler, saying it was 'entirely natural that we should concern ourselves with the question on the European level', expatiated on this too:

> The Jew must leave Europe! At best they'll go to Russia. I have no sympathy. They always stir people up against each other. They do it in public as much as in private life. They'll also have to quit Switzerland and Sweden. There, where they are few, they are at their most dangerous. In no time at all five thousand Jews in Sweden occupy all the leading positions. But this makes it all the easier to remove them![18]

Notes

1. J. Walk (ed.), *Das Sonderrecht für die Juden im NS-Staat – Inhalt und Bedeutung* (Heidelberg: Müller, 1981), p.360. See also the Jewish Telegraphic Agency news bulletin, 10 February 1942.

2. B. Lösener, 'Als Referent im Reichsministerium des Innern', in *Vierteljahrshefte für Zeitgeschichte*, 9, 3 (July 1961), p.311.

3. See T. Sandkühler's review of Florent Brayard's *Auschwitz, Enquête sur un Complot Nazi* (Paris: Seuil, 2012). Accessed on 16 February 2021 from: https://www.hsozkult.de/publicationreview/id/rezbuecher-18397.

4. P. Witte et al (eds), *Der Dienstkalender Heinrich Himmlers 1941/42* (Hamburg: Hans Christians Verlag, 1999), entry dated 13 January 1942.

5. R. Hilberg et al (eds), *The Warsaw Diary of Adam Czerniakow* (New York: Stein and Day, 1979), entry dated 19 January 1942.

6. *Tages-Post*, 20 January 1942.

7. See C. Gerlach, 'The Wannsee Conference, the Fate of German Jews, and Hitler's Decision in Principle to Exterminate All European Jews', in *The Journal of Modern History*, 70, 4 (December 1998), p.779.

8. R. Breitman, *Official Secrets – What the Nazis Planned, What the British and Americans Knew* (New York: Hill and Wang, 1998), p.111.

9. See his testimony before the International Military Tribunal on 8 April 1946, *Trial of the Major War Criminals before the International Military Tribunal*, XI (Nuremberg: 1947), pp.50-4 and in The Ministries Case in 1948-49 (*Trials of War Criminals before the Nuernberg Military Tribunals*, XIII (Washington, DC: US Government Printing Office, 1952), pp.414-21. In the first, when he was a witness for the defence, he said he had seen a summary of what was said at Wannsee. In the second, when he too was on trial, he denied receiving a copy. See M. Roseman, *The Villa, the Lake, the Meeting* (London: Allen Lane/Penguin, 2002), p.77.

10. Hence Kritzinger's subsequent comment to another member of the Reich Chancellery that the criteria would result in a '*Hornberger Schiessen*' or non-solution (Yad Vashem Shoah Resource Center, 'An Interview with Prof. Hans Mommsen', December 1997. Accessed on 16 February 2021 from: http://www.yadvashem.org/odot_pdf/Microsoft%20Word%20-%203850.pdf.

11. Only one copy of the 15-page Wannsee protocol has ever been found. Its discovery in 1947 was enough to condemn Bühler to death in a Polish court in 1948.

12. *The Irving Judgment* (London: Penguin, 2000), p.144.

13. A decree published in the *General Gouvernement* on 21 January 1942 on the terms of employment of Jews withdrew the right to overtime pay, reduced the legal period of notice to one day and stipulated that women and children were exempt from any legal coverage (*Goniec Krakowski*, 22 January 1942). For an in-depth discussion of German labour legislation in Poland, see D. Majer, '*Non-Germans*' under the Third Reich (Baltimore, MD: John Hopkins University Press, 2003).

14. See Roseman, *The Villa, The Lake, The Meeting*, p.77. Roseman has also written a thought-provoking paper on the way the Wannsee conference has been reinterpreted over time as new evidence has emerged and new research approaches have been applied, in H-C. Jasch and C. Kreutzmüller (eds), *The Participants – The Men of the Wannsee Conference* (2017), pp.21-39.

15. A. Mayer, *Why Did the Heavens Not Darken?* (New York: Pantheon, 1989), pp.285-6.

16. W. Jochmann (ed.), *Adolf Hitler – Monologe im Führerhauptquartier 1941-1944* (Hamburg: Knaus, 1980), entry dated 25 January 1942.

17. One German estimate, at this time, was that only 1 million of the 3.9 million Soviets captured since June 1941 were still alive. Hitler refused to allow Red Cross assistance to POW camps. See in the Donovan Nuremberg Trials Collection the staff evidence analysis of Nuremberg document number 1201-PS, p.24. Accessed on 16 February 2021 from: https://lawcollections.library.cornell.edu/nuremberg/catalog/nur:00701.

18. See Jochmann (ed.), *Adolf Hitler – Monologe*, entry dated 27 January 1942. Author's translation.

12

Win or Lose

At the end of January, Hitler addressed another rally at the *Berliner Sportpalast,* on this occasion to celebrate the ninth anniversary of his party's coming to power. He used it to convey the message that Germany must ready itself for drastic action.

In a disjointed delivery, interrupted by frequent bursts of applause, he emphasised how Germany was in a similar position to the one it had faced in the Great War, up against a world of enemies bent on German subjugation. It was one long conflict which, for him, had never really ended. Taunting Churchill and Roosevelt who, despite his best efforts, had succeeded in their warmongering, he touched upon the 'loquacious' Mr Cripps, the man who had lured the Soviets into a secret alliance with England. That was why Germany had struck first. An unusually cold winter meant his army had had to stand firm and wait. 'The hardest lies behind us'. In the spring they would be ready to retake the offensive. He did still believe in great victories, but they were not guaranteed. What he could promise was that Germany would not be undermined and collapse from within. The enemy powers had not 'won' in 1918. There had been a squalid revolt by a rabble of capitalists, liberals and Marxists, stirred up by 'the eternal Jew', which brought Germany to its knees. Jewish 'cliques' were endeavouring to reproduce these conditions. About the Jews themselves he did not wish to speak, save to say that in 1939 he had given advance warning – and he was 'not one to prophesy lightly' – that the war they were trying to provoke would not turn out the way they were supposing, that it would end instead with their extermination. In spite of his words of caution, war had resulted. The Jews knew the risks they were running and had foolishly put their own lives in jeopardy. 'For the first time', he said with a cold fury, 'it won't be other people who bleed to death' *(verbluten)*. 'This time', adopting the very phrase Goebbels had employed in his November press article, 'the old Jewish proverb will apply: an eye for an eye, a tooth for a tooth!'[1]

He made this brief passage sound like a sudden insertion, a passing remark overshadowed by his ringing plea for an immense increase in the production of 'more and more weapons'. In itself his appeal was an indirect admission that Barbarossa, conceived as a quickfire triumph, had gone wrong.[2] Failure meant it was somebody's fault. There was no mistaking how offended he felt that people had not taken him at his word and that the Jewish race, at least in Europe, had forfeited the right to life. His December speech had referred to German casualties without hinting at an evening up of the losses involved. This speech, strongly influenced by Goebbels, was Hitler's 'authentic voice',[3] foreshadowing the Jewish catastrophe that was being hatched by his collaborators. The war was still winnable. The new Europe was not yet safe. Germany was losing its finest sons. The Jews, whose mischief-making and seditious nature were the primary cause of all the world's troubles, must suffer too. They were not being cleared out swiftly enough. There had to be an 'acceleration', both in timing and in methods, enacted without the slightest compunction.

Rumours about the ascendancy of Himmler and Heydrich added to the impression that something was afoot.[4] The resolution of the Jewish question – this had not been contested – was under the direction of the SS. Heydrich indicated as much by sending a letter to all the commanders and inspectors of the security police and security service across Europe, attaching another copy of his July commission and bringing it to their notice, adding that the requisite preparatory work (i.e. those organisational, practical and financial elements outlined in the *ermächtigung*) had been 'introduced'.[5] By including the leaders of the four main *Einsatzgruppen*, he was making it clear that the 'Final Solution' in the east was part and parcel of the whole project. Eichmann, Heydrich's 'officer-in-charge', was also busy. In a *schnellbrief* or express letter to regional police stations, he recalled the recent evacuations from parts of Greater Germany, which were the 'starting point' for 'the Final Solution of the Jewish Question' in the *Altreich*. They had been modest because of the 'limited absorptive capacity' of the 'reception centres' and difficulties with transportation. New possibilities were currently being looked at with the aim of despatching further contingents. He then summarised the guidelines that were to govern the next stage, particularly regarding the exemptions (Jews employed in protected war industries and Jews over the age of 65, for example), and asked each police station to calculate the number of eligible Jews in their respective areas.[6]

What 'reception centres' was Eichmann considering? We can follow in his footsteps. He had been to Lublinland, Globocnik's fiefdom, in October to survey the site of Belzec. 'Globonik' (sic) meanwhile was being condemned by the BBC in a radio broadcast to Europe in relation to 'horrifying reports' of 'cruelties' towards the Poles and Jews under his protection.[7] Eichmann, post-war, accepted that after quite a long gap he had paid another visit to Lublin in order to see how far Globocnik had advanced. It is Peter Witte's conjecture that Eichmann's second trip was around about the time, and possibly on the eve, of Wannsee.[8] Eichmann was introduced to Hermann Höfle, Globocnik's Chief of Staff who was responsible for 'co-ordinating' Operation Reinhardt, as it came to be called. Höfle took Eichmann back to Belzec where they found a police captain, Christian Wirth, using a large Russian submarine engine to feed exhaust fumes by pipework to a chamber inside a barrack hut. From Eichmann's description, it seems he was being shown a gassing facility, to which Wirth was putting the finishing touches before testing the equipment.[9] Again according to Witte, the Belzec facility will have been one of the 'various possible solutions' discussed at Wannsee.

Other journeys Eichmann made may have been in the same time frame. He went to Chelmno, in the Warthegau, to see a gas van being deployed on Jews brought there from Lodz, witnessing the loading up of the interior, the fifteen-minute journey accompanied, at first, by frantic screams and the eventual unloading of corpses next to a burial pit. Such 'actions' began in December 1941 but only on a larger scale in the second half of January 1942. In a rare public reference to Jewish executions, Gauleiter Arthur Greiser, speaking in Torun, upriver from Chelmno, told his audience that punishment 'was meted out to some thousands of them in a place not far away recently'.[10] Eichmann also travelled to Minsk to attend an open air shooting, describing how, one very cold morning, he arrived as the last victims, among them women and children, were being dispatched. Two witnesses at his trial testified they had seen him at an execution in early March.

Eichmann's trips have baffled historians, raising many suspicions.[11] He freely brought them up in conversation, but there was a blurring of names, dates and locations, and his explanation that they were merely 'informative' is implausible. He reported back to Müller on his findings, stressing the psychological damage being done to members of the SS firing squads, which suggests that he was making a comparative evaluation of the three 'solutions' – the original, by bullet, and the two alternatives of a mobile gas van or a fixed gassing unit that were first mooted the previous autumn. He was actively searching, that is, for a more efficient mechanism for discreetly disposing of greater numbers and at a faster rate.

Quite what Heydrich had meant at Wannsee by 'transit ghettos' is another persisting riddle. Was this a sincerely proposed option at the time he spoke of it, or was it, in all likelihood, part of a cover story designed to mislead?[12] There were several small towns handily clustered around Lublin that, with their rail connections, might serve as 'antechambers' to Belzec.[13] The feasibility of the Lublin scheme for reducing the number of unwanted Jews involved converting the *General Gouvernement*, as Buhler must have understood, from a temporary way-station into a dead-end terminus. In return for helping to solve the Jewish question in Germany, the Jewish question would also be solved by the *General Gouvernement* within its own borders, abolishing the racially unassimilable, Germanising the land with aryan colonists and adding considerably to the 'living space' of the Reich. In February and early March there were many signs that this was exactly what was being pursued. Indigenous Jews were identified and further restrictions placed on their confinement. The *inaptes* had the most to fear. One unconfirmed story was that Warsaw, in an instruction that 'came directly from Hitler', would be flattened and rebuilt, with the Jews in the ghetto carted off lock, stock and barrel to the Lublin 'reservation'.[14]

Some of the able-bodied, as Heydrich mentioned, were assigned to SS construction brigades. An increasing proportion were also meant to be sent, to make up for the diminishing number of Soviet POWs, to closed concentration camps to work on various SS projects, of which arms production was the priority. In late January, Himmler had told Richard Glücks, the head of the Inspectorate of Concentration Camps, to expect the arrival of some 150,000 German Jews in the next four weeks. In fact this promise was not kept. Nevertheless many were directed to Majdanek, a work camp operated by Globocnik on the outskirts of Lublin, and to Auschwitz, in Upper Silesia, 70 kilometres to the west of Krakow. Eichmann is not, at this stage, thought to have gone to Auschwitz. Be that as it may, he did in mid-February begin arranging for the transfer of 20,000 Slovak Jews that Slovakia had been offering to Himmler.

Once the 'protocol' of the Wannsee discussion was finalised, it was stamped with the highest security classification and circulated to 30 recipients. Accompanying the document was a note by Heydrich expressing his pleasure at the 'complete agreement' about the 'basic design' of his plan which had been reached, and inviting the respective subordinates of each State Secretary for further talks about outstanding matters on 6 March, asking that they should contact Eichmann, his 'competent expert'.

This meeting was largely spent re-examining the question of half-Jews and Stuckart's halfway house that they should be compulsorily sterilised, but nothing was settled. Hitler had not, in any case, made up his mind. Eichmann chaired another discussion on the same day with RSHA officers about the forthcoming evacuation of a further 55,000 Jews from the old

Reich and the Protectorate.[15] His redrafted guidelines were now in force to ensure that any Jews exempted from evacuation were not wrongly deported (which had been the case with some of those transported to Riga in October and November, annoying Lohse and Meyer). To 'save face', namely to avoid deporting people who were obviously incapable of heavy labour, elderly Jews were to go to Theresienstadt. Eichmann made a special point of emphasizing that no-one should obtain advance knowledge that deportations were looming, underlining the requirement for 'absolute secrecy'. One at least of the train destinations was Trawniki, a short distance from Lublin.[16] Three days beforehand, the Governor of Lublin had been informed that the authorities in Krakow had given their agreement to the resettlement in his district in the coming month of 14,000 German Jews.[17]

In the third of a series of significant public statements since the turn of the year, a short speech in Munich – read out in his absence – to observe the 22nd anniversary of the founding of the Nazi Party, Hitler played up the historic magnitude of Germany's 'final reckoning of accounts' with those forces, 'Jewish capitalism and communism', intent on splitting up and destroying the German race. National Socialism had conquered many other states and, with their cooperation, his prophecy – the elimination of the Jew – was going to come true. Whatever the outcome of the war, win or lose, and however long it took, this would be the inescapable result. Only the eradication of this 'parasite' would bring a real peace to the world.[18] Goebbels, after reading his copy of the Wannsee protocol, had an equally messianic viewpoint, gratified that Hitler was the driving force behind 'an uncompromising antisemitic attitude'.[19] 'The situation is now ripe for a final settlement of the Jewish question.' They were proceeding 'radically and consistently'. Later generations would lack the willpower or the instinctive alertness to do what was essential.

Notes

1. 'Bleed to death', preferred by Arno Mayer, is a better translation than Burrin's milder 'shed their blood'.
2. A. Milward, *War, Economy and Society 1939-1945* (London: Allen Lane, 1977), pp.55-7.
3. D. Thomson, 'Pogrom Politics', in *The Spectator*, 5 February 1942.
4. *The New York Times*, 10 February 1942.
5. A letter from Heydrich to various security police and *Sicherheitsdienst* (the SD, or security service) officials enclosing a copy of his *ermächtigung*, 25 January 1942.
6. Accessed on 17 February 2021 from: https://www.ghwk.de/fileadmin/Redaktion/PDF/Konferenz/eichmann-schnellbrief.pdf.

7.   *The Palestine Post*, 26 January 1942.

8.   *Die Welt*, 27 August 1999.

9.   Dr Kallmeyer, the T4 specialist, was also in Belzec in February/March 1942.

10.   *The Hebrew Standard of Australasia*, 5 February 1942.

11.   Compare and contrast I. Wojak, *Eichmanns Memoiren* (Frankfurt am Main: Campus Verlag, 2001), C. Gerlach, 'The Eichmann Interrogations in Holocaust Historiography', in *Holocaust and Genocide Studies*, 15, 3 (Winter 2001), pp.428-52 and C. Browning, 'Perpetrator Testimony – Another Look at Adolf Eichmann', in C. Browning (ed.), *Collected Memories – Holocaust History and Postwar Testimony* (Madison, WI: University of Wisconsin Press, 2003), pp.3-36.

12.   This issue is directly addressed in an interesting paper by Jan Erik Schulte (*Die Wannsee-Konferenz im Kontext von SS-Arbeitskräfteplanung und Völkermord 1941/42* (2003)). Accessed on 17 February 2021 from: https://www.ghwk.de/fileadmin/Redaktion/PDF/Jahrestage/2003-schulte.pdf.

13.   R. Kuwalek, 'Die Durchgangsghettos im Distrikt Lublin' in B. Musial (ed.), *'Aktion Reinhardt' – Der Völkermord an den Juden im Generalgouvernement 1941–1944* (Osnabrück: Fibre, 2004), p.198.

14.   The Jewish Telegraphic Agency news bulletin, 3 March 1942.

15.   Report by the Düsseldorf police representative, dated 9 March 1942, of the meeting held at the RSHA on 6 March 1942, reproduced in C. Browning et al, *German Railroads, Jewish Souls: the Reichsbahn, Bureaucracy, and the Final Solution* (New York: Berghahn, 2019), pp.52-53.

16.   'Richtlinien zur technischen Durchführung der evakuierung von Juden in das Generalgouvernement (Trawniki bei Lublin)'(undated). Accessed on 17 February 2021 from: https://www.justice.gov.il/DataGov/Adolf-Eichmann-Records/t1395.pdf.

17.   J. Kielbon, 'Judendeportationen in den district Lublin (1939-1943)', in Musial (ed.), *'Aktion Reinhardt'*, pp.129-30.

18.   *Das Znaimer Tagblatt*, 25 February 1942.

19.   E. Fröhlich (ed.), *Die Tagebücher von Joseph Goebbels*, II, 3 (Munich: K.G. Saur, 1994), entry dated 7 March 1942.

13

Orders

It is undeniably the case, as previous chapters have shown, that Hitler's lethal rhetoric acted as a catalyst in driving forward the 'solution' of the 'Jewish question'. Ever since January 1939, each statement in which he made a special attack on the Jews – responding to alleged threats posed by an international, Jew-inspired conspiracy – had been closely followed by a new package of discriminatory acts.[1] Policy developed in fits and starts and with several flashpoints, which different historians have given various degrees of prominence to. Other factors (such as the Germanic colonising of the east) carried weight, but the fundamental dynamic was Hitler's ramping up of the diplomatic stakes, punishing his antagonists measure for measure. The realising of his prophecy, physically obliterating his one true enemy, was because 'the Jews' themselves, by foiling his attempt to demolish Soviet Russia, forced him into it. Reconstructing who did exactly what is complicated, however, by the secretiveness that had always enveloped the project, the language that was devised to conceal its increasingly annihilationist turn and the desire to distance Hitler from the implementing of his 'wishes'.

Christopher Browning's dictum is a good rule of thumb – if you want to know what Hitler was thinking, you should look at what Himmler was doing.[2] It was Himmler who, at Hitler's behest, activated the intensified assault on Soviet Jewry in July 1941, the resumption of deportations in September and October 1941 and the subsequent authorising of both Greiser and Globocnik. The lines of authority were not always clear cut, nor did they always go unchallenged. The purpose of Wannsee, in a nutshell, was to obtain agreement that Heydrich's plan, however provisional, was to be centrally managed and exclusively controlled by the office of the *Reichsführer*.

Does this suffice to demonstrate that the spring of 1942 was a kind of culmination? Once senior civil servants were squared at Wannsee, did Hitler then, and only then, proceed to take the last fatal step? There were several straws in the wind. Deportations were, though there were still hold-ups, to be substantially expanded. Not, Hitler told Himmler, by eventual transportation to GULAG camps up in the Arctic – the fit and healthy were needed for manning the armaments factories.[3] He had yet to decide about evacuating non-working Jewish family members from Germany, but was under increasing pressure.[4] Goering was also (according to Heydrich) active again, insisting that Jews could only be shipped eastwards 'for annihilation' with his personal approval.[5] Perhaps most pointedly of all, there was considerable unease in many of the ministries that Himmler, armed with his strengthened mandate, was about to swoop. Regarding the Wannsee plan, Lammers had been reserving his position, but, after the second discussion by officials on 6 March, was contacted discourteously by 'some unimportant man' in the RSHA asking for his views.[6] Franz Schlegelberger, in the Ministry of Justice, had been telling Lammers with some anxiety that the proposals pertaining to half-Jews were utterly impracticable. With this in mind, Lammers arranged to report for a second time to Hitler. Once more the *Führer*, according to Lammers, 'cut things short', stating that he did not want to discuss the matter any further while the war was going on. When Lammers also saw Himmler, Himmler – whatever private qualms he may have had – told Lammers he alone was responsible to Hitler, warning Lammers to 'keep your fingers out of this'.[7] Undaunted, Lammers chose to circulate Hitler's 'instructions' in an official note to Goering, Wilhelm Frick, the Minister of the Interior, and to others, stating that Hitler had repeatedly explained he wanted to shelve solving the Jewish question until after the war. Lammers touted it as 'a definite victory over the RSHA', believing it would ensure that 'fundamental decisions are not reached by a surprise intervention from another agency….'[8] It was only some while later that he learned the stop was ineffective and deportations were going ahead.

Was nothing formalized? What of Lammers's 'unimportant man'?

Eichmann, despite his deceptively lowly rank, was someone to be feared. His Berlin office, formerly the home of a Jewish charity, was tightly guarded and inaccessible. That he was 'Himmler's specialist' in the expulsions of Jewry was commonly known, certainly by the end of 1941, and even surreptitiously encouraged. Barbara Stangneth has listed how often he had been referred to in the German and Axis press. Even her probing is not exhaustive. The Swedish *Social Demokraten* newspaper knew right away (see pages 31-32) about the 'full powers' Eichmann was granted in July 1941. Quoting an 'informed' German source at the time the Jewish population of Denmark was at risk in October 1943, the same paper referred to an existing 'Hitlerian decree' ordering that all Jews were to be cleared from Europe, to be acted upon by 'Storm Troop leader Eichmann', the 'Jew dictator'. Whether Germany won or lost the war, the paper's source frankly remarked, not a single Jew and very few Poles would survive. This story was picked up by other transnational news agencies.[9] In early 1944 he was said (accurately in fact) to have been placed under arrest by the SS itself for embezzling the property of murdered Jews.[10] Although, by this stage, claims of a systematic butchering of Europe's Jews were widely spoken about, above all in the United States, the issuing of an official fiat, or anything else for that matter, was still unproven. It seemed improbable that the Nazi hierarchy would have put down on paper, still less preserved, such a damning piece of evidence. Eichmann, at least, was well aware that the Allies, if they ever got their hands on him, would not show him any mercy. In all of the initial war crimes inquiries in 1944-45, he was a wanted man, a key person of interest.[11]

The first individual to provide information about the particulars of Eichmann's wartime career was one of his team of advisers, Dieter Wisliceny, who was attached to the Slovak republic from 1940 to 1943. Wisliceny was captured in May 1945, interrogated and then testified as a star witness for the prosecution at Nuremberg. After that he was handed over to the new Czechoslovakian authorities. Sitting in his cell in Bratislava, he compiled several longhand reports about the development of anti-Jewish oppression by the SS, supplementing these with a character profile of Eichmann and tips as to his likely whereabouts. Keen to implicate his former boss, Wisliceny relied a good deal on hearsay, but he was impressively enlightening about the singular task entrusted to Eichmann by his superiors. Dan Michman for one has set out a very strong argument for re-evaluating Wisliceny's 'richly informative' insights.

Wisliceny claimed to have discovered what was really happening to the Jews of Europe in July or early August 1942 when the Slovak regime, with whom he had negotiated the deportation of some 50,000 of the country's Jewish citizens, began asking for reassurances about their safety.[12] Wisliceny went back to Berlin to see Eichmann, who invited him to his office. In the course of a long and 'serious' talk in which Wisliceny put the case for a visit to the Lublin area of Poland by a Slovak delegation, Eichmann said that this was 'impossible' and after some prevarication told Wisliceny that most of the Slovak Jews were no longer alive. Wisliceny asked who was responsible. Eichmann said that what he was about to tell him he must guard with his life and swear never to reveal to anyone. Eichmann opened his safe, took out a thin file and handed to Wisliceny a sheet of paper with a red border, bearing Himmler's 'unmistakeable signature'. It was addressed to Heydrich and to Oswald Pohl, the head of the SS Main Economic and Administrative Office, or WVHA, stating that

...the *Führer* has decided that the final disposition [sic] of the Jewish question is to begin at once. I [Himmler] designate the Chief of the Security Police and the SD [Heydrich] and the Inspector of Concentration Camps to execute this order. Excluded from this disposition are the Jews needed for the labour programme in the concentration camps. Details about the execution of this order are to be agreed upon by the Chief of the Security Police and the SD and the Inspector of Concentration Camps. About the execution of this order, I am to be continuously informed.

The document, Wisliceny thought from memory, dated from the end of April or the beginning of May 1942. The order he saw, so he understood, was a 'limitation' by Himmler of a slightly earlier, maximalist one – entailing the complete biological extermination of European Jewry – which Hitler had initially enunciated. The file also contained other letters from Himmler to Heydrich. When Wisliceny, in his words, said he hoped to God Germany's enemies would never be in a position to do anything like this to the German people, Eichmann told him not to be sentimental – it was a *Führer* order, and he (Eichmann) had been given full authority by Heydrich in order to achieve 'a first-class performance'. Wisliceny said it struck him that Eichmann, in his meticulous way, had the power to exterminate millions of people in whatever way he considered best. Later on, in 1944, he overheard Eichmann conversing with Rudolf Höss (the former commandant of Auschwitz) and learned further details. The 17,000 unmarried Slovaks, who were fit and healthy, had gone not to Lublin but to Auschwitz to help develop the camp. Of the later batch of 33,000 (i.e. their families), they also went to Auschwitz, but the active were screened out on arrival and the rest were killed in gas chambers using carbon monoxide. On average, the able-bodied represented about one-fifth to one-quarter of all those on the transports.

In one of his written reports in 1946, Wisliceny put together some considered reflections suggesting how the policy of annihilation came about. The war of 1939 was regarded by Hitler and Himmler as a supreme confrontation between the Aryan and non-Aryan peoples, but a sharpening of antisemitism only became evident with the ferocious fighting against the Soviet Union and the moves – accentuated in German home front propaganda – by the United States towards closer involvement. He recalled the July *ermächtigung* which had strengthened Eichmann's status, the marking of Germany's Jews and Goebbels's November article on Jewish guilt, and spelt out the importance of Eichmann's association with Odilo

Globocnik, who invented his own killing 'process'. A virtue of Globocnik's murder-by-gassing was that it was less likely to attract attention, particularly since there had been 'instances' where police units had refused to carry out shootings. Globocnik and Eichmann, between them, drew up a plan of action which was passed up to Himmler and endorsed 'in person' by Hitler. The purpose of the whole programme, Wisliceny heard from Eichmann, was to deliver such a stunning blow to the Jewish race in Europe that it would never recover – an observation which matches the gist, in effect, of what Heydrich had put before his colleagues at Wannsee. Though Wisliceny made no mention of the conference, this was plainly the plan he was talking about. According to Wisliceny's chronology of events, Eichmann must have been in possession of Hitler's order when he began in earnest to arrange the new round of deportations in March 1942.[13]

Wisliceny was not the only prisoner to allude to a specific order. Hans Frank, taking issue with Goering when they were incarcerated in Nuremberg, admitted he had been aware of a 'secret law' concerning the extermination of the Jews, agreed upon by Hitler, Himmler and Heydrich. Höss said he had an interview with Himmler and was told of a directive from the *Führer* to solve the Jewish question 'once and for all'.[14] Wisliceny was exceptional because he testified that he had seen an original order with his own eyes and supplied plenty of incidental, albeit often secondhand information to go with it.[15] His willingness to cooperate was not, in the end, enough to save his own skin. What he did do, in his last memorandum, was to leave behind a shortlist of those individuals who were in a position to corroborate his account and provide extra 'clarity'. There were three of them – Heinrich Müller, who had vanished; Eichmann, probably in hiding in his native Austria[16]; and, failing these two, the aforementioned Pohl, who had been found and taken into custody in May 1946.

What did Eichmann and Pohl have to say for themselves?

Eichmann's many versions of his own story, before and after he was eventually apprehended in Argentina in 1960, were strongly coloured by what he called Wisliceny's 'cowardly', 'distorted' accusations. It had never been in his power to 'direct' the destruction of Europe's Jews. He had not had a *vollmacht*. He could not initiate or influence policy. The Wannsee plan was not 'his' plan. Others had always decided. This applied, most of all, with regard to Hitler, whose every wish had the force of law. 'The whole world' knew of Hitler's repeated pronouncements about the consequences of a full-blown 'Jewish' war. When it became clear that the conquering of Russia would not be a walkover, all restraints fell away. Eichmann maintained, telling the same anecdote over and over again, that he was sent for by Heydrich, who had just come from Himmler, who had received a deliberate order from Hitler to carry out the physical extermination of the Jews. Heydrich's 'little speech' took Eichmann by complete surprise. Such a 'violent' solution had never occurred to him. Having said that, he did not entirely reject Wisliceny's account. An order was issued and passed on to him orally. He accepted that there 'could' have been a second, slightly altered written order by Himmler, suitably rather than crudely phrased.[17] He also conceded that he was not just an 'ordinary' recipient of commands; he was committed to his task and was the 'right' person for the role. He was wounded by the disloyalty of Wisliceny, but he did not wish to rule out the idea that he may well have briefed his advisers about his exploratory trips in the early weeks of 1942.[18]

Eichmann's suggestive encounter with Heydrich has attracted plenty of interest. A frequent reaction is one of disbelief, laced with jibes about the credulousness of others. Yet the snag is not, as might be imagined, that Eichmann was making it up. An affidavit by Wilhelm Höttle, who served in the *Sicherheitsdienst*, adds credence to Eichmann's assertions. On the basis of a conversation Höttle had with Eichmann in August 1944 about his annihilation operations, Eichmann said 'that Heydrich had given him these directives'.[19] The real drawback with Eichmann's tale is putting a date to it. In the Sassen tapes, recorded when Eichmann was at liberty in Argentina, Heydrich's announcement took place at 'the turn of the year 1941/42'. Interviewed by Avner Less, an Israeli police officer, Eichmann said it was some two or three months after the outbreak in June 1941 of the German-Russian war. At other times he spoke about the meeting having occurred in the 'late fall' of 1941. True or not, by chopping and changing his mind he made his own account very hard to verify or to refute. The prosecutors at his trial had no reason to even try. Raul Hilberg, the doyen of Holocaust historians, put his finger on the cardinal point. 'The most important question remains: when did Eichmann first hear that Hitler had ordered the physical elimination of the Jews? When was that?'[20]

In his anxiety to acquit himself of the charge that he was a heartless monster, Eichmann made one insistent observation. All he had done, he averred, was to deliver the Jews for deportation. From then on his involvement had ended. Heydrich had been quite clear about it. The RSHA would not have anything to do with the dirty work. Its role was only concerned with policing, assembling and transferring Jews to particular locations, mainly railway stations, where they would then be taken away to the camps in Lublin or elsewhere. Oswald Pohl, the man who presided over the WVHA, was 'uniquely responsible' for the labour requirements and running of the concentration camp system. This was the alibi that Eichmann clung to.

Pohl, the third of Wisliceny's leads, was Himmler's chief administrator, the manager of the SS's sprawling industrial works and, among Himmler's famous 'circle of friends', the one person to have his 'absolute and unlimited trust'.[21] Proficient in finance and personnel matters, he had extensive dealings with Globocnik and was familiar with the latter's special duties. But Pohl, as Himmler appreciated, had a much more professional attitude to the construction and engineering challenges involved in the Germanisation of the eastern territories and knew how to 'supervise' the use of concentration camp inmates for various projects. Early in 1942, with Hitler pushing for a rapid increase in munitions, mobilising Jewish labour would, for Himmler, make the SS's enterprises an integral part of the war economy.[22] On 1 February Pohl's two main offices, for Administration and for Budget and Building were merged into a single body, the WVHA, unifying the organisational structure. The death on 8 February of Fritz Todt, the economics minister, and the appointment in his place of Albert Speer, created the opportunity to streamline and rationalise wartime production. To utilise slave labour potential to the full, Himmler – having discussed it with Hitler[23] – initiated a further reform, removing the Inspectorate of Concentration Camps (the ICC) from Heydrich's control and placing it under Pohl. In so doing, the camps lost their earlier, punitive function and were reconfigured to underscore their economic value. Heydrich must have been displeased but Müller played down the snub because the transfer, he acknowledged, 'serves the direction of the war effort'.[24]

After Germany's surrender in 1945, Pohl hid from the Allies, passing himself off as a farm labourer. When he was eventually caught he attempted to take cyanide and was badly beaten by his British captors. His arrest dominated the headlines, the press describing him as the 'creator' of the gas chambers in Auschwitz, carrying out 'Hitler's policy of "extermination through work"'.[25] Within a week he was being cross-questioned under oath. His interrogators asked him about when and how the concentration camps were transferred to his organisation. Pohl's replies were sketchy. He had been to see Himmler about another matter, and Himmler had only brought up the issue towards the end, explaining that the war was reaching its 'climax' and he had been talking with Speer about the best way of effecting the boost in armaments Hitler was counting on. Instead of parcelling out concentration camp manpower in a piecemeal fashion, Himmler wanted it to be done more methodically, asking armaments firms to submit their needs to a head office tasked with their overall deployment. He asked Pohl to take on the job, saying he had nobody else who could do it. Pohl resisted, reminding Himmler that he already had many managerial burdens, but Himmler would not budge, proposing – as a trade-off – to transfer the ICC to the WVHA while letting Richard Glücks, the existing Inspector of the ICC, remain in day-to-day charge. Reluctantly, Pohl agreed to handle the 'economic side'. He confessed that he 'knew' about 'the so-called Final Solution of the Jewish Question'. It was 'a question of state' and 'could only have been discussed between Himmler and Hitler'. The authorisation for gassing actions was, he believed, passed down from Himmler to Müller and Eichmann, whom 'everybody knew had the power', and then to Glücks. All of this commenced at 'the beginning of 1942', whereas he had only assumed the responsibility for the camps much later in 'the summer' of that year. His meetings with Glücks, he said, only occupied one hour a week of his time. His policy was always to retain (keep alive) more inmates in order to fulfil the demands of industry. He, for his part, had had nothing to do with the extermination programme.[26]

At the end of each day of interrogation, Pohl was seen by a prison psychiatrist. Notes of their conversations surfaced in 2006.[27] Although he covered much of the same ground, Pohl was slightly more talkative. He had 'protested' when Himmler had suggested he take the ICC under his wing, but his protests were ignored. However he had 'stipulated' that he would only handle the 'administering' of the camps. Glücks was the one to whom Himmler assigned the execution of the 'Final Solution'. He, Pohl, had 'demanded' this of Himmler. He had 'stayed out of it'. His role was strictly limited to the allocation of labour.

Pohl was interviewed on numerous further occasions, the questioning switching to his participation in the pillaging and disposal of valuables belonging to Jewish deportees. In July, he was presented with the documentary evidence – a photostat of a letter of his to Himmler – referring to 'your order of March 3rd 1942' about officially attaching the ICC to the WVHA, flatly contradicting his defence that it had been later on in the summer of that year. Pohl, lamely, explained the order was not put in writing but was delivered to him 'man to man' and only became fully operational in May. As his questioner told him, 'you know this is important'.[28]

And so it is. Postwar, Pohl and then Eichmann passed the buck to each other, using the haziness of the chain of command to obscure their own liability. Their buck-passing, for our purposes, is immaterial. Their accounts conflict, but that conflict provides a vital glimpse of an answer to Hilberg's query. Himmler's ICC order to Pohl was coterminous with an extermination order that Hitler had lately given to Himmler. The transfer of the ICC can be dated with some precision to the first few days of March 1942.[29]

With a secure date to go by, we also obtain a clearer notion of the sequencing of subsequent, associated orders. It is best to think in terms of a twin-track undertaking.[30]

The order that Eichmann heard about from Heydrich specifically applied, at any rate in the first place, to Globocnik's activities. Globocnik had already been informed by Himmler, to whom he was directly answerable. Belzec was the designated camp for the clearing of the *General Gouvernement*. It was purely exterminatory, relatively small and makeshift, staffed by technicians from T4 and a minimal team of orderlies. To stop Frank from interfering, Himmler called him before a three-man inquisition and accused him of corruption and personal extravagance. Frank was forced to agree to the appointment of Friedrich-Wilhelm Krüger (Himmler's Higher Police chief in Krakow) as the official State Secretary for security in the *General Gouvernement*, giving Himmler unimpeded control of the kind he had obtained in the occupied eastern territories, though Frank tried to suggest that all police measures would need his prior consent.[31] Himmler arrived in Krakow on 13 March and gave a speech outlining how to populate and slice up parts of Poland with new German racial stock[32], promising that one-half of the Jews in the *General Gouvernement* would be evacuated by the end of 1942.[33] He went on to Lublin the following day to confer with Globocnik. Acting as a 'courier', Eichmann then made his own way to see Globocnik to deliver the permission to dispose of a first instalment of 250,000 Jews, for which – Eichmann recalled – Globocnik had insisted on having written confirmation. On the night of 16-17 March, the Lublin ghetto was emptied and 1,400 Jews who were deemed to be 'unemployed' were taken by train, under armed guard, to Belzec. The camp, in a secluded clearing in thick woodland, connected by a spur to the main railway line, had been altered to resemble a stopover station. The Jewish labourers who helped to construct the surrounding fencing and barbed wire had already been the first victims. The new arrivals from Lublin were now gassed. Regular convoys continued for four further weeks, topped up by many from Lvov. Höfle brushed aside questions from other offices by saying that those heading to Belzec, all of them *arbeitsunfähig*, were to 'cross the frontier and never return to the *General Gouvernement*'.[34] Jews deported from Germany arrived and were 'resettled' in villages dotted around the Lublin area at the same time. By early April, a second similar camp was under construction at Treblinka, north-east of Warsaw.

Auschwitz emerged in parallel with but distinct from the Globocnik camps. Because of its location and transport links it was ideally located to receive the Jews of western and southern Europe, both to accommodate and to annihilate. Plans to enlarge and extend the site had already been submitted in February, shortly before Pohl's meeting with Himmler. Pohl, after an introductory talk with Speer's staff, went to Auschwitz as part of a tour of the fifteen concentration camps that were now under his authority. He faithfully put into practice Himmler's tenet that, given the urgent state of the war and the acute labour shortage, it was justifiable to 'exploit even the dying efforts of anyone and everyone to achieve victory'.[35] In his appraisal and outline of future work which he sent to Himmler at the end of April, he advised camp commanders to treat their camps from then on as economic enterprises, maximising output for 'war purposes', and that the employment of available labour 'must be, in the true meaning of the word, exhaustive...'.[36] It was this advice which Himmler accepted and which necessitated his written, revised order – the one Wisliceny was shown by Eichmann – for the able-bodied to be 'excluded' from the 'Final Solution', much to the annoyance of Heydrich.[37] Eichmann, in the Sassen tapes, can be heard saying that 'the whole business did not take the form originally laid down in the *Führerbefehl* since it turned out that all able-bodied Jews were put to work and as such stayed alive'.[38] A letter written by Heinrich Müller in mid-May, mentioning a 'general order' by Himmler to exempt Jews aged between 16 and 32 from 'special measures' until further notice, supports this narrative.[39]

It is true that the earliest arrivals in Auschwitz, several thousand Slovak Jews, survived for some months. One cannot infer from this, though, that all the decisions of major significance to do with a fully *European*-scale solution were actually only taken in the summer, rather than the spring, of 1942. Wisliceny answered the point. The job of the first Slovak contingent was to build the larger facilities for those who were to come after them. The account by Höss adds a further detail. The construction of a fenced off women's barracks stemmed, he said, from the time of the order for the retention of the physically active, 'since the need for a women's camp in Auschwitz only arose as a result of this order'.[40] Work on putting up that camp began in March.

Several general conclusions can be drawn.

Wisliceny was a truthful 'insider'. The soundness of his timeline is borne out by cross-comparing the declarations of the two protagonists whose names he volunteered. In contradicting each other, Pohl and Eichmann confirmed when and by what means the transmission of an original Hitler order and, a little later, a second one by Himmler, took place. Wisliceny's lead supplies the basis for believing, with some confidence, that we are eavesdropping on the crucial exchanges.

Knowing when assists in grasping the motive. Hitler's harking back in public to his 'prophecy' was anything but histrionic. The war had not been – his promise – 'completed'. The Jews were to blame for frustrating Germany's 'fight for existence' and must be made to pay in full. Heydrich's Wannsee plan, which was Eichmann's own work, envisaged a phased extinguishing of Jewry over an unspecified period (with a Globocnik component). But this depended on victory, which was no longer assured. A second capitulation, restoring 'Jew-power' in German Europe, was unthinkable. The Jews had to be deported and dealt with rapidly and conclusively while Germany was still in a position to do it.[41] Himmler's contribution, counselled by Pohl, was to persuade Hitler to allow a stay of execution, a deferral, for Jews fit enough to be worked to death. The 'worthless' were to be dispatched forthwith.

How is it that this dating was not detected long ago? After all, parts of Wisliceny's report were in print by the mid-1950s. The Pohl and Eichmann cases created a mountain of testimonies and affidavits, full of investigative pointers. Their most personally damaging comments, however, were conveniently disowned. Pohl's first interrogations became valueless when, after being indicted in January 1947 along with several other members of the WVHA, he retracted most of the statements he had previously made, arguing that he had only learned about the extermination programme in late 1943.[42] Similarly, a ruling at Eichmann's trial meant that most of the bulky transcript of what he told Sassen was inadmissible in court. In the last decade or so, with the advent of online publication of a great quantity of documents recording and commemorating the Holocaust, these scattered fragments – a full releasing of Wisliceny's Slovak reports by the Yad Vashem centre, of the initial questioning of Pohl by his American interrogators (available on an American commercial site since 2009) and Chapter IV of Eichmann's reminiscing with Sassen – have become readily retrievable and can be juxtaposed, helping to crack open the conundrum.

That Hitler, if he gave any order, only did so verbally, is a strongly-held opinion in most academic circles. Nor would there be any written evidence of this kind had it not been for Pohl's influencing of Himmler. Pohl's promotion to the rank of *Obergruppenführer* – approved by Hitler on 17 March 1942[43] – put him on a par with Heydrich and gave him the authority to match his extra responsibilities. From then on, it was his job to exploit to the utmost those Jews who were 'interrupting' their journey 'to the east'. As one of Himmler's 'bearers of secrets' – the 80 or so individuals sworn to carry out the 'Final Solution' in complete secrecy[44] – Pohl was perfectly well aware of 'what I owe my destiny to'.

Notes

1. See the comment by Eichmann in *The Trial of Adolf Eichmann*, 7 (Jerusalem: Trust for the Publication of the Proceedings of the Eichmann Trial: Israel State Archives, 1995), p.186.
2. Yad Vashem Shoah Resource Center, 'An interview with Prof. Christopher Browning' (1997), p.10. Accessed on 18 February 2021 from: http://www.yadvashem.org/odot_pdf/ Microsoft%20Word%20-%203848.pdf.
3. C. Gerlach, 'The Wannsee Conference, the Fate of German Jews, and Hitler's Decision in Principle to Exterminate All European Jews', in *The Journal of Modern History*, 70, 4 (December 1998), p.799.
4. S. Willems, *Der Entsiedelte Jude – Albert Speers Wohnungsmarktpolitik für den Berliner Hauptstadtbau* (Berlin: Edition Hentrich, 2002), quoting from Goebbels's diary. This exemption was eventually annulled in May.
5. See the interrogation of Friedrich Jeckeln in G. Fleming, *Hitler and the Final Solution* (Berkeley and Los Angeles, CA: University of California Press, 1984), p.97, recalling the contents of a letter he had received from Heydrich in February 1942.
6. *Trials of War Criminals before the Nuernberg Military Tribunals*, XIII (Washington, DC: US Government Printing Office, 1952), especially p.416.
7. Lammers interrogation, 23 October 1945, in the Donovan Nuremberg Trials Collection. Accessed on 18 February 2021 from: https://lawcollections.library. cornell.edu/nuremberg/catalog/nur:01753.
8. Quoted in R.J. Evans, *Telling Lies about Hitler – The Holocaust, History and the David Irving Trial* (London: Verso, 2002), p.89.
9. For example *The Lewiston Daily Sun* of 8 October 1943. Rolf Günther, Eichmann's deputy, had been sent to Copenhagen to oversee the rounding up of Denmark's Jewish population.
10. *The Palestine Post*, 1 March 1944.
11. See the CIA files, released in 2005, which are held at the US National Security Agency, especially Documents 4, 6, 7 and 8 in Volume 1 of the Directorate of Operations. Accessed on 19 February 2021 from: https://nsarchive2.gwu.edu/NSAEBB/NSAEBB150/ index.htm.
12. Interrogation of Dieter Wisliceny on 15 November 1945 in the Donovan Nuremberg Trials Collection. Accessed on 19 February 2021 from: http://lawcollections.library. cornell.edu/nuremberg/catalog/nur:00769.
13. D. Wisliceny, 'Die Bearbeitung der jüdischen Probleme durch die Sicherheitspolizei und den Sicherheitsdienst' (report dated 18 November 1946) in the Yad Vashem Archives, Record Group M.5 File 162. Accessed on 19 February 2021 from: https://documents.yadvashem.org. Note that Rudolph Kastner, who had dealings with

Eichmann and Wisliceny in 1944-5, was given a slightly different account by Wisliceny, who told him that Aichmann (sic) had summoned his advisers to Berlin *in the spring of 1942* and informed them that there had to be 'a speedy disposal of the Jews of Europe', to be carried out 'silently' in gas chambers. Speed was essential, since 'after the war it will not be possible to utilise such methods' (see Document 2605-PS, the affidavit of Dr Rezso (Rudolph) Kastner, in *Trial of the Major War Criminals before the International Military Tribunal*, XXXI ((Nuremberg: 1948)), pp.1-15). It is not a trivial discrepancy. Did Wisliceny hope to hide from the Slovaks that he had had foreknowledge of the fate awaiting the Slovak Jews?

14. Höss stated that this interview took place in June 1941. Katrin Orth ('Rudolf Höss und "Die Endlösung der Judenfrage" – Drei Argumente gegen deren Datierung auf den Sommer 1941', in *Werkstatt Geschichte* (1997)) 18, pp.45-57, has proved otherwise.

15. Michman argues that many observers in the early postwar years were too quick to dismiss what Wisliceny had to say ('Täteraussagen und Geschichtswissenkraft – Der Fall Dieter Wisliceny und der Entscheidungsprozess zur "Endlösung"' in J. Matthäus and K-M. Mallman (eds), *Deutsche, Juden, Völkermord – Der Holocaust als Geschichte und Gegenwart* (Darmstadt: Wissenschaftliche Buchgesellschaft, 2006), pp.205-19. A slightly updated and translated version can be found in the *Journal of Contemporary Antisemitism*, 1, 2 (Spring 2018), pp.15-32.

16. Wisliceny's Nuremberg testimony had been widely published in January 1946. Eichmann, detained in a POW camp under a false name, made his escape immediately afterwards and went on the run.

17. J. von Lang (ed.), *Eichmann Interrogated – Transcripts from the Archives of the Israeli Police* (London: The Bodley Head, 1983), pp.267-8.

18. *Ich, Adolf Eichmann – Ein historischer Zeugenbericht* (Leoni am Starnberger See: Druffel-Verlag, 1980), in particular pp.175-84 and 229-35. The book is a heavily-edited printing of his memoirs by a German lawyer, Rudolf Aschenauer, taken from the tapes made by Sassen. The visits Eichmann made *could*, therefore, have been in the January-February-March phase.

19. *Trial of the Major War Criminals before the International Military Tribunal*, XI (Nuremberg: 1947), p.257.

20. *Die Welt*, 28 August 1999.

21. P-F. Koch, *Himmlers Graue Eminenz – Oswald Pohl und das Wirtschaftsver waltungshauptamt der SS* (Hamburg: Verlag Facta Oblita, 1988), p12.

22. M. Thad Allen's *The Business of Genocide – The SS, Slave Labour and the Concentration Camps* (Chapel Hill, NC: University of North Carolina Press, 2002), especially Chapter 5, is a thorough study of the competing interests in play.

23. D. Eichholtz, *Geschichte der Deutschen Kriegswirtschaft 1939-1945*, I (Berlin: Saur, 2003), p.222. This is confirmed by Albert Speer in *The Slave State – Heinrich Himmler's Masterplan for SS Supremacy* (London: Weidenfeld and Nicolson, 1981), p.22.

24. 'Integration of the office of the ICC into the SS Main Office', 30 May 1942. Accessed on 19 February 2021 from: http://nuremberg.law.harvard.edu/documents/3927-circular-notice-to-the-security?q=*#p.1.

25. *Die Weltpresse*, 29 May 1946; *Wiener Zeitung*, 30 May 1946.

26. Fold 3 Historical Military Records (https://www.fold3.com/), World War II Nuernberg Interrogation Records digitised from the US National Archives (3 June 1946), pp.9-11, 19-25; (4 June 1946), pp.53-5, 63-4; (7 June 1946), p.17; (8 June 1946), p.12; (13

June 1946), p.22. For open access copies see the Thomas J. Dodd papers in the Archives and Special Collections of the University of Connecticut Digital Archive (Series VII, Subseries D, Defendant Files, Funk, Walter)(https://archivessearch.lib.uconn.edu/repositories/2/resources/771). Also Pohl's autobiographical essay of 23 July 1946 in the Yad Vashem Archives, Record Group O.23, File 39. Accessed on 19 February 2021 from: https://documents.yadvashem.org.

27. L. Goldensohn, *The Nuremberg Interviews* (London: Pimlico, 2006), pp.395-414.

28. Fold 3 Historical Military Records (10 July 1946), pp.1-3.

29. Himmler's desk diary indicates that he saw Pohl at Friedrichsruh, his own forward HQ not far from Rastenberg, on 6 March 1942. Entries for the 4th and the 7th make it clear that their discussion was about Pohl's 'taking over' of the *Konzentrationlagers*. See P. Witte et al (eds), *Der Dienstkalender Heinrich Himmlers 1941/42* (Hamburg: Hans Christians Verlag, 1999).

30. Chapter 6 of Nikolaus Wachsmann's *KL: A History of the Nazi Concentration Camps* (London: Little, Brown, 2015) neatly draws together the ordered and the disorderly elements of this stage of decision-making, although, as Dieter Pohl notes in 'Die "Aktion Reinhard" im Licht der Historiographie', in B. Musial (ed.), *'Aktion Reinhardt' - Der Völkermord an den Juden im Generalgouvernement 1941–1944* (Osnabrück: Fibre, 2004), pp15-47, there is not much consensus among historians about these matters.

31. Excerpt from Frank's diary of 18 March 1942, in *Nazi Conspiracy and Aggression*, IV (Washington, DC: US Government Printing Office, 1946), pp.910-1.

32. Note of a confidential talk by Himmler in *Nazi Conspiracy and Aggression*, III (Washington, DC: US Government Printing Office, 1946), pp.640-1.

33. A news item by the Jewish Telegraphic Agency news bulletin on 20 March 1942 reported that Himmler had issued instructions to the security police in many parts of Poland and the occupied east to 'reduce' their Jewish populations, using as a reason their presence as a 'hindrance' to the German army in sensitive border areas.

34. C. Ajenstat et al, *H. Höfle - l'Autrichien artisan de la Shoah en Pologne* (Paris: Berg International, 2006), pp.139-40.

35. Message by Pohl, quoting Himmler, dated 13 March 1942, from the Bundesarchiv Koblenz (NS 3/1080), re-quoted in J. Tuchel, *Die Inspektion der Konzentrationslager 1938-1945 - das system des terrors* (Edition Hentrich, 1994), p.22 and p.88.

36. Pohl to Himmler, 30 April 1942, in the Donovan Nuremberg Trials Collection. Accessed on 19 February 2021 from: https://nuremberg.law.harvard.edu/documents/2928-report-to-heinrich-himmler.

37. Heydrich died in early June after being wounded in an attempted assassination in Prague, just weeks after the issuing of the second order.

38. See page 10 of the extract from the Sassen manuscript (Section IV) originally uploaded onto the website of David Irving in 2010. Accessed on 19 February 2021 from: www.fpp.co.uk/Auschwitz/Eichmann/Eichmann_IV.pdf. Sassen's tape recordings are held in the German Federal Archive in Koblenz.

39. D. Pohl, 'Die grossen Zwangsarbeitslager der SS – und Polizeiführer für Juden im Generalgouvernement 1942-1945' in U. Herbert, K. Orth and C. Dieckmann (eds), *Die Nationalsocialistischen Konzentrationslager – Entwicklung und Struktur*, I (Göttingen: Wallstein Verlag, 1998), footnote p.434.

40. R. Höss, *Commandant of Auschwitz* (London: Orion, 2000), p.189.

41.   Robert Ley (in charge of the German Labour Front) reportedly said that though Germany 'was conducting war on various fronts, the principal war aim was directed against the Jews, and hence Germany was determined to go on fighting until the destruction of Jewry was achieved' (*The Jewish Chronicle*, 13 March 1942).

42.   An annihilation order, he claimed, had never ever passed through his hands (quoted in *Der Spiegel*, 31 May 1947). See also his signed affidavit of 31 March 1947 (Nuremberg document NO-2618) held by the Wiener Library (Collection reference 1655, Reference number 1655/2657). One attendee in court wrote of Pohl's 'dark, almost gipsy complexion, piercing eyes, hardened features, cruel mouth and air of an animal of prey', denying 'everything' (R. Kastner, 'Le procès d'un chacal', in *Socialisme*, January 1948). After a failed appeal he was hung in 1951.

43.   Noted in P. Witte et al (eds), *Der Dienstkalender Heinrich Himmlers 1941/42* (Hamburg: Hans Christians Verlag, 1999), entry dated 17 March 1942.

44.   See the notes of a talk in 1957 with Gottlob Berger, one of Himmler's closest SS collaborators, in the archive of the Institut für Zeitgeschichte, Munich (ZS-0427_2). Accessed on 19 February 2021 from: https://www.ifz-muenchen.de/archiv/zs/zs-0427_2.pdf.

14

Who Knew?

The sub-dividing of functions between the WVHA and the RSHA signified the precise organisational point at which the 'Final Solution' took on a genocidal form. A tight clique of SS officers occupied key positions in the machinery of destruction, sternly overseen by Himmler. A few privileged figures were also in the know. One such was Joseph Goebbels.

Dictating his diary on the morning of the 27 March 1942, Goebbels briefly recorded the lull in fighting in the Far East (Java, a Dutch colony, had just fallen to the Japanese), British attempts to buy Indian support for the war and the latest twists in American propaganda. 'Beginning in Lublin', he then wrote in one continuous paragraph:

> ...the Jews under the *General Gouvernement* are now being evacuated eastward. The procedure is pretty barbaric and is not to be described here more definitely. Not much will remain of the Jews. About 60 per cent of them will have to be liquidated; only about 40 per cent can be used for forced labour. The former *Gauleiter* of Vienna, who is to carry out this measure, is doing it with considerable circumspection and in a way that does not attract too much attention. Though the judgment now being visited upon the Jews is barbaric, they fully deserve it. The prophecy which the *Führer* made about them for having brought on a new world war is beginning to come true in a most terrible manner. One must not be sentimental in these matters. If we did not fight the Jews, they would destroy us. It's a life-and-death struggle between the Aryan race and the Jewish bacillus. No other government and no other regime would have the strength for such a global solution as this. Here, once again, the *Führer* is the undismayed champion of a radical solution, which is made necessary by existing conditions and is therefore inexorable. Fortunately a whole series of possibilities presents itself to us in wartime which would be denied us in peace. We shall have to profit by this. The ghettos that will be emptied in the cities of the *General Gouvernement* will now be refilled with Jews thrown out of the Reich.

This process is to be repeated from time to time. Jewry has nothing to laugh about, and the fact that Jewry's representatives in England and America are today organising and sponsoring the war against Germany must be paid for dearly by its representatives in Europe – that is only right.

These remarks, found amongst papers salvaged from the rubble of the Reich Propaganda Ministry in 1945, first appeared in print in 1948.[1] Somebody must have tipped Goebbels off. He knew about Belzec. He knew, not much more than ten days after the 'barbaric' gassing had begun, of the task assigned to Globocnik, 'the former *Gauleiter* of Vienna'. He knew of the elaborate logistics involved in how the unspeakable processing was being done – retaining only the able-bodied and emptying and refilling the ghettos – and of the terminology to hide what the clearance 'to the east' entailed. He knew – he openly understood – that 'liquidation' meant killing. But, though he connected it to Heydrich's 'global' scheme and the manpower requirements of the war economy, his real justification was to boil it all down to the same prophesying of Hitler which was coming to pass 'in a most terrible manner'. Nazi Germany had had enough of the Jews. Those of them in England and the US who were pulling the strings were out of reach. Their confederates in Europe would get their just desserts. The regime had the boldness to solve this whole question. At its head stood Hitler, 'the undismayed champion of a radical solution'.

It is unlikely that Hitler was Goebbels's informant. Hitler preferred to threaten and harangue in a generalised way even in front of his associates. And yet, in a single graphic passage, quoted in full as it must be, Goebbels provided the strongest proof of Hitler's guiding hand. Hitler, Eberhard Jäckel concludes from this diary entry, was the chief originator of 'this bloody work', drummed home by the 'monstrous obstinacy' of his repeated menaces.[2] Goebbels, digesting the 'horror' of what he had learned, according to Martin Broszat, was applauding Hitler for being the main inspirer.[3] The passage is 'explicit evidence' (in Hugh Trevor-Roper's view) that Hitler was directly responsible.[4] Many other documents show Hitler intervening in Jewish affairs on several occasions in late 1941 and early 1942. None of them are quite as incriminating.

If a study of Himmler's activity is worthwhile, then so too are the comings and goings of Goebbels.

Hitler's address to the Munich gathering was a cold-blooded pledge that the Jews of Europe would not survive the war. Himmler, Bormann and Goebbels had all been together in the audience. Over the course of the following week, Goebbels received a report on the security situation in occupied Russia which recorded a flaring up of partisan actions and elicited from Goebbels the crushing response that the more the Jews were eliminated, by whatever means, the better. Glancing through his copy of the Wannsee protocol, he endorsed the solving of the Jewish question 'within a pan-European frame', either by concentrating them in the east or possibly isolating them on a distant island. On a speaking tour of Austria, he also groused about Jewish émigrés in Britain who were in cahoots with Churchill in promising for the future a 'free' and 'independent' Austria.[5] Then, on the 13 March in its weekly digest of foreign news items, the London-based *Jewish Chronicle* ran a front-page 'statement' in 'the Nazi press' by Goebbels,

> ...regretting the German Government's past action in allowing tens of thousands of Jews to leave countries under the control of Germany to become the principal 'war agitators' in Britain and America. But, say the Nazis, the Jews, especially those locked up in the ghettos, are entertaining false hopes if they believe that a defeated Germany will bring them relief. Germany, they declare, has the means of destroying the Jews whenever it may be found necessary, and the last bullets and poison gas will be kept in reserve for the realisation of Hitler's prophecy that this war is to result in the destruction of the Jews so that they can never again celebrate a victory over Germany.[6]

Evidently drawing on the same third-party source, Jewish papers in the United States cited the Jewish Press Service in Geneva:

> Venting his rage upon the escaped German Jewish refugees who now lie outside the heavy hand of Nazi rule, and attributing the war agitation against the Reich to them, Reich Propaganda Minister Paul [sic] Goebbels expressed sharp regret that the Nazis had let these persecuted victims emigrate, according to the Nazi newspaper, the Hacken Kreutz Banner. Whatever the ultimate decision of the war, Goebbels promised, ghetto Jewry would meet destruction. The Nazis, Germany's minister of hate threatened, intended their destruction, even using poison gas, to eliminate their hated victims.[7]

These snippets help to contextualise the entry in Goebbels's diary. He understood that gas was about to be used and anticipated that the ghettos were to be targeted. He also felt, the story suggested, that the previous encouragement of emigration had been a grievous error. This rings true. Kersten refers to Himmler's original preference for letting the Jews go abroad and his complaint that Goebbels, aided by Bormann, had gained the upper hand and talked Hitler into opting for extermination – all of which accounts for the gloating tone.[8] What Goebbels did was to ensure that eliminationist propaganda worked in favour of what eventually became an eliminationist policy.

The catch with the Geneva report is that there was no such 'statement' by Goebbels, either in the *Hakenkreuzbanner* newspaper or put out by any other official German news outlet.[9]

The information about Goebbels's actual views could have been picked up from gossip or whispers, giving it a shine of credibility by attributing it to a provincial newspaper. The chances are, however, that it was put into circulation by his ministry, part of one last attempt to scare the British and Americans.[10] Geneva, after all, was an important listening post in neutral Switzerland. Diplomats were well aware of Goebbels's leaking to further his 'nefarious ends', provoking an Allied response so that he could paint the UK and the US as the agents of Jewish power.[11]

In any event, there was a trickle of stories indicating that the Nazi approach of increasing persecution was giving way to a much more concerted programme. The head in Geneva of the Jewish Agency for Palestine, Richard Lichtheim, was one of the most observant onlookers. Apprised of Heydrich's idea to group together all of the remaining Jews in the Protectorate in Theresienstadt where, Lichtheim judged, they would be 'slowly starved', he was the first to obtain a sense of a 'plan' to deport and destroy Germany's Jews 'before the war is finished'.[12] News of the transfer of Slovakian Jews to 'a ghetto near the Polish border' led him to make representations to the papal nuncio in Switzerland about a larger risk of extermination extending to 'millions' of Jews even in countries associated with but not actually occupied by Germany. Added to this was a growing apprehension that Germany's so-called labour conscription (*arbeitseinsatz*) scheme was little more than a smokescreen.[13] Chaim Weizmann – the leading Zionist and a particular *bête noire* of Goebbels – though more cautious in his estimates than Lichtheim, expressed his fears in his correspondence with the British government in March. He was, he wrote to Viscount Cranborne, the British Secretary of State for the Colonies, pinning his faith in the victory of the United Nations as the surest route to survival, 'for in the matter of exterminating the Jews', Weizmann lamented, 'Hitler is as good as his word'.[14]

Notes

1. L.P. Lochner, *The Goebbels Diaries 1942-1943* (New York: Doubleday and Co, 1948).
2. E. Jäckel, *David Irving's Hitler – A Faulty History Dissected* (Port Angeles, WA: Ben-Simon Publications, 1993). Accessed on 20 February 2021 from: http://www.nizkor.org/hweb/people/i/irving-david/jackel/jt-1-5.html.
3. M. Broszat, 'Hitler und die Genesis der "Endlösung" – Aus Anlass der Thesen von David Irving', in *Vierteljahrshefte für Zeitgeschichte*, 25, 4 (October 1977), p.763.
4. *The Sunday Times*, 12 June 1977.
5. *Welt Blatt*, 13 March and 15 March 1942.
6. *The Jewish Chronicle*, 13 March 1942. The same article spoke of a German radio report in which the spokesman said Hitler had turned the annual Jewish celebration of Purim over the 'Aryans' into a day of mourning, particularly for those in the ghettos, and that 'he meant to see to it that the Jews should never be able to celebrate it again'.
7. *Ohio Jewish Chronicle*, 13 March 1942; *The Chicago Sentinel*, 26 March 1942.
8. F. Kersten, *The Kersten Memoirs 1940-1945* (London: Hutchinson, 1956), p.163.
9. Microfilm copies of the *Hakenkreuzbanner* newspaper are held by the *Stadtarchiv* of Mannheim.
10. The Berlin correspondent of the *Hakenkreuzbanner*, Johann von Leers (a prolific Nazi ideologue), worked in Goebbels's ministry.
11. The US administration was certainly coy when it came to commenting on German atrocities, often preferring to talk of the victimising of 'certain populations'. Many suspected it did not want to give the impression that it was the tool of 'Jewish-capitalist interests' of Hitler's imagination.
12. R. Cohen, 'Confronting the reality of the Holocaust: Richard Lichtheim, 1939-1942', in *Yad Vashem Studies* XXIII (1993), p.336.
13. L. Rothkirchen, 'Vatican Policy and the "Jewish Problem" in "Independent" Slovakia' (1939-1945) in M. Marrus (ed.), *The Nazi Holocaust, Part 8 – Bystanders to the Holocaust*, 3 (Berlin: de Gruyter, 1989), p.1319.
14. Weizmann to Lord Cranborne, letter dated 6 March 1942, reproduced in H. Friedlander and S. Milton (eds), *Archives of the Holocaust*, 4 (New York: Garland, 1990), p.370.

Epilogue
The Reason Why

Human understanding of historical events is cursed by a nagging indeterminacy. The documentary record is always incomplete. Greater distance and perspective do not necessarily help. The past escapes us. The inception of the 'Final Solution' – an historian's problem *par excellence* – was a murky and perplexing occurrence, aspects of which defy comprehension. Nonetheless, what drives the quest for new and significant answers, greatly facilitated by the rise of digitised history, is 'the uncovering of some final truth'.[1]

The principal purpose of the present study has been to bring together the empirical evidence concerning Hitler's self-proclaimed 'prophecy' – the circumstances in which it was initially expressed and circulated; how it motivated the desire, as a truly worldwide war took shape, to punish the Jews by separating and then ejecting them from German-held territory; and its demonstrable linkage to the eventual, homicidal activation of the machinery of death. The 'prophecy' is the key to the Holocaust, the study argues, since it explains when and why a defining order was, or rather orders were, put into practical effect.

The 'prophecy', at source, represented a unilateral move by Hitler to weaponise the 'Jewish problem' as an international issue. Hitler's public stance was one of peace with menaces. Germany's own Jews had been defeated, dispossessed and had in the main left the country. He intended to use the Aryanisation (plundering) of wealth to develop Germany's own very extensive sphere of economic interests. Small though it was, the remaining Jewish presence in Germany was all the more unacceptable. The Western democracies must take in Jewish refugees in far greater numbers, or else Germany would address the matter on its own terms, imposing a 'reign of terror'. And if Jewish opinion-leaders thought they could incite others to go to war to obstruct Germany's natural aspirations, the Jewish race in Europe – captive and exposed – would be destroyed. This threatening statement, puzzling to so many, was elaborated on in comments he made before a private audience of army and business experts (which also came to the notice of US diplomats).[2] To attain economic self-sufficiency, it was vital for Germany to also secure the industrial and agricultural resources of the European continent. Since important parts of the European economy were in Jewish hands, their controlling position had to be broken up. The essential point was not, as Germany had mistakenly done in the Great War, to confront these enemies all at once. The 'dollar Jews' would be outsmarted; the threat to Jewish lives in Europe would be enough to inhibit America from intruding once again in European affairs. The war which Hitler started, supposedly to pre-empt Jewish plotting, opened with the successful occupation of Poland and, just months later, the emphatic defeat of France, isolating Britain. To bring unwelcome British resistance to an end, he meant to round things off by crushing the Soviet Union while holding the United States at bay, leaving him free to unify Europe and deal with the Jews at his leisure.

Anti-Jewish policy evolved in step with the military position. After Poland was overrun, tens of thousands of German Jews were transported to an out-of-the-way reservation in eastern Poland, some of them even being prodded across the border into Russia. Following the collapse of France, a proposal to establish a Jewish statelet in one of France's colonial possessions took hold, to be run under German 'supervision' and as a guarantee of American good behaviour. Nothing had come of this, however, by the time of the launching of Barbarossa. Several million more Jews lay in the path of the German advance. The intention was always to eradicate the Judeo-Bolshevik backbone of the Soviet regime, but the viciousness of partisan warfare gave Hitler the excuse – despite denials – to widen the slaughter to the non-combatant Jewish population. This too justified clamping down on German and other European Jews, for whom a total plan of relocation in former Soviet territory (emigration from Europe having all but dried up) was now being readied in expectation of final victory. Once Britain and the United States, ignoring Hitler's vow to retaliate, had come out in full support of the Soviet cause, the alignment of 'Jewish' capitalism with 'Jewish' communism, accompanied by the stirring up of dissidents in German-occupied territory, lent credence to his 'prophecy'. Making preparations for the partial evacuation of Jews from some of Germany's biggest cities – Goebbels pushing Hitler into it just after the release of Churchill and Roosevelt's Atlantic Charter – was an obvious warning shot to Roosevelt and 'the Jewish war-agitators' advising him.

The immediate difficulty was finding destinations where Jewish convoys could be sent in the interim. Some were moved up to the *Ostland* (including Minsk), where SS firing squads were operating. In other localities gas vans were introduced to reduce the number of uneconomic Jews resident in ghettos, making way for German arrivals. But it was an unco-ordinated process, confusing many eastern administrators, without any strong central direction. It also alarmed the higher civil service, leading to accusations of foot-dragging. With German troops closing in on but unable to take Moscow, the US Senate's repeal of the Neutrality Act provoked Goebbels into a furious counterblast in which he called Jews 'the enemy's agents among us', admonished officials for holding things up and committed the regime to 'irreversibly' solving the Jewish question without further delay.[3]

Japan's attack on Pearl Harbor and Hitler's almost automatic declaration of war on the United States brought into being the two-front war he had hoped to avoid. A Soviet winter offensive heightened the sense of crisis, momentarily shaking the High Command. Hitler's desire for revenge, blaming the Jews for triggering the conflict and then extending it, was overpowering. The Wannsee conference secured the support of officials for a relatively long-term resettlement and exploitation of Jewish labour from the whole of continental Europe, but Hitler, since time was pressing and the outcome of the war so uncertain, wanted a speedier and deadlier course of action. After preliminary testing, the first extermination centres opened in the *General Gouvernement,* designed to mop up Polish Jewry. Alongside this project a broader plan was concocted, under SS management, around the simultaneous drive to produce the vast scale of munitions needed to continue the war, setting up workshops in camps – particularly Auschwitz – designated to receive the Jews of southern and western Europe, the able-bodied being worked to exhaustion while the unproductive excess was quietly disposed of. In speeches and statements in this same period – the first few months of 1942 – Hitler and his acolytes made it known in broad, non-specific terms that the Jews were suffering a fate that he had repeatedly warned about and was richly deserved, penalising the perpetrators by redeeming a promise made to the German people, the rest of the world and, not least, to the Jews themselves.

Hitler – with Goebbels the hardliner and Himmler a more hesitant executor – was the moving force behind this unfolding cataclysm. His recorded sayings at critical points have the greatest possible probative value. Everything hinged for him on overthrowing the Soviet Union by force of arms before the British and still more the Americans could come to the aid of the Soviets. To help to discourage them, he countered each Allied move by taking stronger action against the Jewish populations in his grip, advertising his resolve. These hurried initiatives, in what was a fluid and volatile setting, illustrate just how contingent they were. Had Moscow fallen and the Soviet Union succumbed, an all-out exterminationist programme would not have arisen. The final 'Final Solution' was, above all, circumstantial. Infuriatingly denied a military triumph, anxious about the climbing German loss of life, fearing uprisings of the same sort that cost Germany in 1918 – all these considerations combined to create a headlong rush forwards. 'The Jewish question' was to have been settled when and only when the war, brief in duration, was won. Instead, the lengthening conflict provided the gruesome 'necessity' for – much more drastically – solving it.

The crime of the century was, so Hitler would have it, the consummation of a far-sighted prediction, the unerring prognosis of an infallible prophet.[4] This – if we recall – was what lay behind the self-serving, staggering affirmation of his last testament, when, staring defeat in the face, he maintained the real culprits responsible for the war, foolishly discounting his clear warning, had received their 'due punishment'. In reality it was the product of a failed enterprise, a reckless gamble that Nazi Germany could win the war by limiting it to Europe.[5] Hitler's increasingly frenzied invoking of his 'prophecy' was his way of making it clear who would have to pay for his own monumental miscalculation.

Notes

1. R.J. Evans reviewing Philippe Sands's *East West Street* in *The Guardian Review*, 9 July 2016.
2. Ambassador Bullitt to Sumner Welles and to President Roosevelt, in *Foreign Relations of the United States*, 1939, General, 1 (Washington: US Government Printing Office, 1956), Document 718, dated 19 September 1939 but also referring to an earlier telegram of 25 March 1939. Accessed on 22 February 2021 from: https://history.state.gov/historicaldocuments/frus1939v01/d718.
3. Christian Barth, author of *Goebbels und die Juden* (Paderborn: Ferdinand Schöningh, 2003), while accepting Goebbels's prominence at this point, thinks of his role as one of obedient compliance to Hitler's will. Accessed on 22 February 2021 from: https://digi20.digitale-sammlungen.de/de/fs1/object/display/bsb00044118_00001.html.
4. The delirious nature of this strain of thinking is set out at greater length by Norman Cohn in his *Warrant for Genocide* (New York: Harper and Row, 1967), especially Chapter VIII.
5. *United States Foreign Broadcast Information Service* daily report, 24 January 1942, summarising a broadcast by Goebbels.

Select Bibliography

Official Papers

Akten zur Deutschen Auswärtigen Politik – 1918-1945, D, XIII, 2 (Göttingen: Vandenhoeck & Ruprecht, 1970)

Bayerische Staatsbibliothek (*Erklärung des Generalfeldmarschalls von Hindenburg vor dem Parlamentarischen Untersuchungsausschuß ['Dolchstoßlegende']*, 18 November 1919: http://www.1000dokumente.de/index.html?c=dokument_de&dokument=0026_dol&object=pdf&st=&l=de

Deutsches Reichsgesetzblatt, I (1941)

Documents on German Foreign Policy 1918-1945, D, XII (Washington, DC: US Government Printing Office, 1962); XIII (Washington, DC: US Government Printing Office, 1954)

Foreign Relations of the United States, 1939, General, 1 (Washington: US Government Printing Office, 1956): https://history.state.gov/historicaldocuments

Führer Conferences on Naval Affairs (Annapolis, MD: Naval Institute Press, 1990)

German History in Documents and Images: http://germanhistorydocs.ghi-dc.org/sub_document.cfm?document_id=1548

Israeli Ministry of Justice (Adolf Eichmann records)

Nazi Conspiracy and Aggression, III (Washington, DC: US Government Printing Office, 1946), IV (Washington, DC: US Government Printing Office, 1946), VII (Washington, DC: US Government Printing Office, 1946): https://www.loc.gov/rr/frd/Military_Law/NT_Nazi-conspiracy.html

Sontag, R. and Beddie, J. (eds), *Nazi-Soviet Relations 1939-1941* (Washington DC, US Department of State, 1948)

The Donovan Nuremberg Trials Collection, Cornell University: http://lawcollections.library.cornell.edu/nuremberg/catalog/

Harvard University Nuremberg Trials Project: https://nuremberg.law.harvard.edu

The National Archives of the UK: War Office

The Niskor Project: www.nizkor.com/hweb/people/e/eichmann-adolf/transcripts/

The Nuremberg Trials Project: https://nuremberg.law.harvard.edu/

The Trial of Adolf Eichmann, 4 (Jerusalem: Trust for the Publication of the Proceedings of the Eichmann Trial: Israel State Archives, 1993), 7 (Jerusalem: Trust for the Publication of the Proceedings of the Eichmann Trial: Israel State Archives, 1995)

Trial of the Major War Criminals before the International Military Tribunal, XI (Nuremberg: 1947), XXV (Nuremberg: 1947), XXVIII (Nuremberg: 1948), XXXI (Nuremberg: 1948)

Trials of War Criminals before the Nuernberg Military Tribunals, XIII (Washington, DC: US Government Printing Office, 1952)

United States Foreign Broadcast Information Service daily reports (British Library)
US National Archives, M1019 – Records of the U.S. Nuernberg War Crimes Trials
Interrogations (1946-1949), Interrogation Report No.2636a, 6 February 1948, pp.1-2
(Courtesy of the Hoover Institution Library, Stanford University)
US National Security archives

Other Archives

Fold 3 Historical Military Records: https://www.fold3.com/
Friedlander, H. and Milton, S. (eds), *Archives of the Holocaust*, 4 (New York: Garland, 1990)
Haus der Wannsee-Konferenz: https://www.ghwk.de/wannsee-konferenz/dokumente-zur-wannsee-konferenz/
Institut für Zeitgeschichte, Munich: www.ifz-muenchen.de
The British Library, *BBC Monitoring Reports* (1941)
The University of Connecticut Archives and Special Collections (the Thomas J Dodd papers): https://archivessearch.lib.uconn.edu/repositories/2/resources/771
The Wiener Library
The website of David Irving: www.fpp.co.uk
US Holocaust Memorial Museum, Holocaust Encyclopedia: https://collections.ushmm.org/search/catalog/irn1000273
Yad Vashem Archives, Record Group TR.3, File 1193; Record Group M.5 (Documentation Centre of the Central Union of Jewish Communities in Bratislava, File 162; Record Group O.23 (G.Gilbert, Nuremberg Collection), File 39: https://documents.yadvashem.org

Diaries

Fröhlich, E. (ed.), *Die Tagebücher von Joseph Goebbels*, II, 1 (Munich: K.G. Saur, 1996); II, 2 (Munich: K.G. Saur, 1996); II, 3 (Munich: K.G. Saur, 1994)
Gilbert. G., *Nuremberg Diary* (New York: Farrar, Straus and Company, 1947)
Goldensohn, L., *The Nuremberg Interviews* (London: Pimlico, 2006)
Hilberg, R. et al (eds), *The Warsaw Diary of Adam Czerniakow* (New York: Stein and Day, 1979)
Hoppe, B. and Glass, H., *Die Verfolgung und Ermordung der europäischen Juden durch das nationalsozialistische Deutschland*, 7 (2011)
Karny, M. et al (eds), *Deutsche Politik im 'Protektorat Böhmen Und Mähren' unter Reinhard Heydrich 1941-1942: Eine Dokumentation* (Berlin: Metropol, 1997)
Matthäus, J. and Bajohr, J. (eds), *The Political Diary of Alfred Rosenberg* (Lanham, MD: Rowman & Littlefield, 2015)
War Journal of Fritz Halder, VII: http://cgsc.contentdm.oclc.org/cdm/singleitem/collection/p4013coll8/id/3974/rec/3
Witte, P. et al (eds), *Der Dienstkalender Heinrich Himmlers 1941/42* (Hamburg: Hans Christians Verlag, 1999)

Newspapers, Magazines and Journals

Miscellaneous

Der Spiegel; Die Welt; Die Zeit; Geschichte und Gesellschaft; History and Memory; History Today; Holocaust and Genocide Studies, La Vie des Idées, Le Monde Diplomatique; The Economist; The (Manchester) Guardian; The Observer; The Spectator; The Times and The Sunday Times; The Times Literary Supplement; The Washington Post; Vierteljahrshefte für Zeitgeschichte; Vingtième Siècle; Yad Vashem Studies
Malmö stadsarkiv: *Dagens Nyheter*
The British Library: *Berliner Börsen-Zeitung, Der Angriff; Der Berliner Börsen-Courier; Ceske Slovo; Deutsche Allgemeine Zeitung; Lidove Noviny; The Jewish Chronicle; The New York Times; Venkov; Völkischer Beobachter*
The Institut für Stadtgeschichte, Mannheim: *Hakenkreuzbanner*
The Kungliga Bibliloteket, Stockholm, Sweden: *Social Demokraten*

Online

ANNO Zeitungen (Austrian Newspapers Online): http://anno.onb.ac.at/:*Das Kleiner Volksblatt; Das Vorarlberger Tagblatt; Das Znaimer Tagblatt; Die Kreuzzeitung; Die Salzburger Wacht; Die Weltpresse; Kleine Volks-Zeitung; Neues Wiener Tagblatt; Neuigkeits Welt-Blatt; Tages-Post; Volks Zeitung; Welt Blatt; Wiener Kronen-Zeitung*
Berliner Zeitung: https://www.berliner-zeitung.de/archiv
Bibliothèque Nationale de France: https://gallica.bnf.fr/html/und/presse-et-revues? mode=desktop:*Le Bulletin Périodique de la Presse Allemande; Le Journal des Débats Politiques et Littéraires; Le Temps; Paix et Droit; Politix*
Bulletin des Fritz Bauer Instituts: https://www.fritz-bauer-institut.de/einsicht
Commentary: https://www.commentarymagazine.com/
Europeana: https://www.europeana.eu/en/collections/topic/18-newspapers?page=1&qf= COUNTRY%3A"Germany"&view=grid&api=fulltext: *Hamburger Anzeiger*
Google Historic Newspapers: https://news.google.com/newspapers: *The Lewiston Daily Sun; The Milwaukee Journal; The Observer-Reporter; The St Petersburg Times (Florida)*
Historical Jewish Press: http://web.nli.org.il/sites/jpress/english/pages/default.aspx: *The Chicago Sentinel; Hamashkif; The Palestine Post*
The Jagiellonian Digital Library: https://jbc.bj.uj.edu.pl/dlibra/publication/83?language= en#structure: *Goniec Krakowski*
Jewish Telegraphic Agency daily news bulletins: https://www.jta.org/archive
Le Journal de Genève and *La Gazette de Lausanne*: https://www.letempsarchives.ch/
The Ohio Jewish Chronicle: https://www.ohiomemory.org/digital/collection/ojc/search
Trove Newspapers: https://trove.nla.gov.au/newspaper/: *The Argus; The Hebrew Standard of Australasia; The Rotarian; The Sydney Morning Herald; The Telegraph (Brisbane)*

Secondary Works

Adam, U., *Judenpolitik im Dritten Reich* (Düsseldorf: Droste Verlag, 1972)

Ajenstat, C. et al, *Hermann Höfle – l'Autrichien artisan de la Shoah en Pologne* (Paris: Berg International, 2006)

Aly, G., *Endlösung – Völkerverschiebung und der Mord an den europäischen Juden* (Frankfurt a. M.: Fischer Verlag, 1998)

G.Aly et al (eds), *Biedermann und Schreibtischtäter* (Berlin: Rotbuch Verlag, 1987)

Aly, G. and Heim, S., *Vordenker der Vernichtung* (Hamburg: Hoffmann and Campe, 1991)

Arendt, H., *Eichmann in Jerusalem* (New York: The Viking Press, 1963)

Barth, C.T., *Goebbels und die Juden* (Paderborn: Ferdinand Schöningh, 2003): https://digi20.digitale-sammlungen.de/de/fs1/object/display/bsb00044118_00001.html

Benz, W., Kwiet, K. and Matthäus, J. (eds), *Einsatz im 'Reichskommissariat Ostland'* (Berlin: Metropol, 1998)

Boehm, E., *We Survived* (New Haven, CT: Yale University Press, 1949)

Bräutigam, O., *So hat es sich zugetragen* (Würzburg: Holzner Verlag,1968)

Brayard, F., *Auschwitz, Enquête sur un Complot Nazi* (Paris: Seuil, 2012)

Breitman, R., *Official Secrets – What the Nazis Planned, What the British and Americans Knew* (New York: Hill and Wang, 1998)

Browning, C., *Nazi Policy, Jewish Workers and German Killers* (Cambridge: Cambridge University Press, 2000); *The Origins of the Final Solution: the evolution of Nazi Jewish policy, September 1939-March 1942* (Lincoln, NE: University of Nebraska Press, 2004); Browning, C. et al, *German Railroads, Jewish Souls: the Reichsbahn, Bureaucracy, and the Final Solution* (New York: Berghahn, 2019),

Burgess, S., *Stafford Cripps – A Political Life* (London: Gollancz, 1999)

Burrin, P., *Hitler et les Juifs – Genèse d'un génocide* (1989); *Ressentiment et Apocalypse – Essai sur l'antisémitisme nazi* (Paris: Seuil, 2004)

Cesarani, D. (ed.), *The Final Solution – origins and implementation* (London and New York: Routledge, 1994); *Final Solution: The Fate of The Jews 1933-49* (2015)

Cohn, N., *Warrant for Genocide* (New York: Harper and Row, 1967)

Domarus, M., *Hitler: Speeches and Proclamations 1932-1945*, 1 (I.B. Tauris, 1990)

Eichholtz, D., *Geschichte der Deutschen Kriegswirtschaft 1939-1945*, I (Berlin: Saur, 2003)

Ich, Adolf Eichmann – ein historischer zeugenbericht (Leoni am Starnberger See: Druffel-Verlag, 1980)

Epstein, C., *Model Nazi – Arthur Greiser and the Occupation of Western Poland* (Oxford: Oxford University Press, 2012)

Erickson, J. and Dilks, D. (eds), *Barbarossa: the Axis and the Allies* (Edinburgh: Edinburgh University Press, 1994)

Evans, R.J., *Telling Lies about Hitler – The Holocaust, History and the David Irving Trial* (London: Verso, 2002)

Falls, C., *Was Germany Defeated in 1918?* (Oxford: Clarendon Press, 1940)

Fleming, G., *Hitler and the Final Solution* (Berkeley and Los Angeles, CA: University of California Press, 1984)

Fraser, L., *Germany Between Two Wars– A Study of Propaganda and War Guilt* (London: Oxford University Press, 1944)

Gerwarth, R., *Hitler's Hangman – the Life of Heydrich* (New Haven, CT: Yale University Press, 2011)

Görlitz, W. (ed.), *The Memoirs of Field-Marshal Keitel* (London: Kimber, 1965)

Hayes, P., *Why? Explaining the Holocaust* (New York: W.W. Norton and Company, 2017)

Heinemann, J., *Hitler's First Foreign Minister – Constantin Freiherr von Neurath* (Los Angeles, CA: University of California Press, 1979)

Herf, J., *The Jewish Enemy – Nazi Propaganda during World War II and the Holocaust* (Cambridge, MA: Harvard University Press, 2006)

Hilberg, R., *The Destruction of the European Jews* (Chicago, IL: Quadrangle Books, 1961); *The Politics of Memory* (Chicago: Ivan R. Dee, 1996)

Hinsley, F. et al, *British Intelligence in the Second World War – its Influence on Strategy and Operations*, 1 (London: HMSO, 1979)

Höss, R., *Commandant of Auschwitz* (London: Orion, 2000)

Huss, P., *The Foe We Face* (Garden City, NY: Doubleday, Doran and Co, 1942)

Husson, E., *Heydrich et la Solution Finale* (Paris: Perrin, 2008)

The Irving Judgment (London: Penguin, 2000)

Jäckel, E., *David Irving's Hitler – A Faulty History Dissected* (Port Angeles, WA: Ben-Simon Publications,1993)

Jochmann, W., (ed.), *Adolf Hitler – Monologe im Führerhauptquartier 1941-1944* (Hamburg: Knaus, 1980)

Kershaw, I., *Hitler 1936-45: Nemesis* (London: Allen Lane, 2000); *Hitler's Place in History* (Open University lecture, 2005): http://www.open.edu/openlearn/history-the-arts/history/ou-lecture-2005-transcript; *Fateful Choices: Ten Decisions that Changed the World, 1940-1941* (London: Allen Lane, 2007); *Hitler, the Germans and the Final Solution* (Yale, CT: Yale University Press, 2008)

Kersten, F., *The Kersten Memoirs 1940-1945* (London: Hutchinson, 1956)

Koch, P-F., *Himmlers Graue Eminenz – Oswald Pohl und das Wirtschaftsverwaltungshauptamt der SS* (Hamburg: Verlag Facta Oblita, 1988)

Kogon, E. et al, *Les Chambres à Gaz – Secret d'Etat* (Paris: Minuit, 1984)

Klein, P., *Die 'Gettoverwaltung Litzmannstadt' 1940 bis 1944* (Hamburg: Hamburger Edition, 2009)

Lanzmann, C., *Le Lièvre de Patagonie* (Paris: Gallimard, 2009); *Le Dernier des Injustes* (Paris: Gallimard, 2015)

Longerich, P., *The Unwritten Order – Hitler's Role in the Final Solution* (Stroud: Tempus, 2001); *Holocaust – the Nazi Persecution and Murder of the Jews* (Oxford: Oxford University Press, 2010); *Heinrich Himmler* (Oxford: Oxford University Press, 2012)

Lozowick, Y., *Hitler's Bureaucrats – The Nazi Security Police and the Banality of Evil* (London and New York: Continuum, 2000)

Lower, W., *Nazi Empire-Building and the Holocaust in Ukraine* (Chapel Hill, NC: University of North Carolina Press, 2005)

Majer, D., *'Non-Germans' under the Third Reich* (Baltimore, MD: John Hopkins University Press, 2003)

Mayer, A., *Why Did the Heavens Not Darken?* (New York: Pantheon, 1989)

Milward, A., *War, Economy and Society 1939-1945* (London: Allen Lane, 1977)

Musial, B. (ed.), *'Aktion Reinhardt – Der Völkermord an den Juden im General gouvernement 1941-1944* (Osnabrück: Fibre, 2004)

Poliakov, L., *Bréviaire de la Haine – Le IIIe Reich et les Juifs* (Paris: Calmann-Levy, 1951)

Rees, L., *Auschwitz: the Nazis and the Final Solution* (London: BBC, 2005); *The Holocaust: A New History* (London: Penguin, 2017)

Reitlinger, G., *The Final Solution* (London: Vallentine, Mitchell, 1953)

Roseman, M., *The Villa, the Lake, the Meeting* (London: Allen Lane/Penguin, 2002)

Rossi, A., *The Russo-German Alliance* (London: Chapman and Hall, 1950)

Rüger, J. and Wachsmann, N. (eds), *Rewriting German History – New Perspectives on Modern Germany* (Basingstoke: Palgrave Macmillan, 2015)

Sandkühler, T., *'Endlösung in Galizien': der Judenmord in Ostpolen und die Rettungsinitiativen von Berthold Beitz 1941–1944* (Bonn: Dietz, 1996)

Sands, P., *East West Street* (London: Weidenfeld and Nicolson, 2016)

Schleunes, K., (ed.), *Legislating the Holocaust – the Bernhard Loesener Memoirs* (Boulder, CO: Westview, 2001)

Schulte, J.E., *Zwangsarbeit und Vernichtung: Das Wirtschaftsimperium der SS* (Paderborn: Ferdinand Schöningh, 2001)

Speer, A., *The Slave State – Heinrich Himmler's Masterplan for SS Supremacy* (London: Weidenfeld and Nicolson, 1981)

Stangneth, B., *Eichmann before Jerusalem – the unexamined life of a mass murderer* (London: The Bodley Head, 2014)

Suppan, A., *Hitler-Benes-Tito* (Vienna: Austrian Academy of Sciences Press, 2014)

Thad Allen, M., *The Business of Genocide – The SS, Slave Labour and the Concentration Camps* (Chapel Hill, NC: University of North Carolina Press, 2002)

Trevor-Roper, H., *The Last Days of Hitler* (London: Macmillan, 1947); Trevor-Roper, H. (ed.), *Hitler's Table Talk* (London: Weidenfeld and Nicolson, 1953)

Tuchel, J., *Die Inspektion der Konzentrationslager 1938-1945 – das system des terrors* (Berlin: Edition Hentrich, 1994)

von Lang, J. (ed.), *Eichmann Interrogated – Transcripts from the Archives of the Israeli Police* (London: The Bodley Head, 1983)

Wachsmann, N., *KL: A History of the Nazi Concentration Camps* (London: Little, Brown, 2015)

Walk, J. (ed.), *Sonderrecht für dir Juden im NS-Staat – Inhalt und Bedeutung* (Heidelberg: Müller,1981)

Welch, D., *Germany and Propaganda in World War 1 – Pacifism, Mobilization and Total War* (London: I.B. Tauris, 2014)

Willems, S., *Der Entsiedelte Jude – Albert Speers Wohnungsmarktpolitik für den Berliner Hauptstadtbau* (Berlin: Edition Hentrich, 2002)

Wojak, I., *Eichmanns Memoiren* (Frankfurt am Main: Campus Verlag, 2001)

Articles

Aronson, S., 'Die dreifache Falle – Hitlers Judenpolitik, die Alliierten und die Juden', in *Vierteljahrshefte für Zeitgeschichte*, 32, 1 (January 1984), pp.29-65

Bauer, Y., 'Who was responsible and when? Some well-known documents revisited' in *Holocaust and Genocide Studies*, 6, 2 (June 1991), pp.129-49

Brayard, F., '"A exterminer en tant que partisans" – sur une note de Himmler', in *Politix*, 2008/2 (no.82), pp.9-37: https://www.cairn.info/revue-politix-2008-2-page-9.htm

Breitman, R., 'What Chilean diplomats learned about the Holocaust': https://www.archives.gov/iwg/research-papers/breitman-chilean-diplomats.html (20 June 2001)

Broszat, M., 'Hitler und die Genesis der "Endlösung" – Aus Anlass der Thesen von David Irving', in *Vierteljahrshefte für Zeitgeschichte*, 25, 4 (October 1977), pp.739-75

Browning, C., 'Zur Genesis der "Endlösung" – eine Antwort an Martin Broszat', in

Vierteljahrshefte für Zeitgeschichte, 29, 1 (January 1981), pp.97-109; 'Perpetrator Testimony – Another Look at Adolf Eichmann', in Browning, C. (ed.), *Collected Memories – Holocaust History and Postwar Testimony* (Madison, WI: University of Wisconsin Press, 2003), pp.3-36

Burrin, P., 'Le génocide des juifs en débats', in *Le Monde Diplomatique*, June 1997, p.26

Cohen, R., 'Confronting the reality of the Holocaust: Richard Lichtheim, 1939-1942', in *Yad Vashem Studies* XXIII (1993), pp.335-68

Friedländer, S., 'From Anti-Semitism to Extermination' (1984): https://www.yadvashem.org/untoldstories/documents/studies/Saul_Friedlander.pdf)

Gerlach, C., 'The Wannsee Conference, the Fate of German Jews, and Hitler's Decision in Principle to Exterminate All European Jews', in *The Journal of Modern History*, 70, 4 (December 1998), pp.759-812; 'The Eichmann Interrogations in Holocaust Historiography', in *Holocaust and Genocide Studies*, 15, 3 (Winter 2001), pp.428-52

Herf, J., 'The "Jewish War": Goebbels and the Antisemitic Campaigns of the Nazi Propaganda Ministry', in *Holocaust and Genocide Studies*, 19, 1 (Spring 2005), pp.51-80

Jersak, T., 'Die Interaktion von Kriegsverlauf und Judenvernichtung: ein Blick auf Hitler's Strategie im Spätsommer 1941', in *Historische Zeitschrift* 268 (April 1999), pp.311-74

Kastner, R., 'Le procès d'un chacal', in *Socialisme*, January 1948, pp.8-14

Kampe, N., 'Besprechung über der Judenfrage – Das Protokoll der Wannsee-Konferenz am 20 Januar 1942': https://www.fritz-bauer institu.de/fileadmin/editorial/publikationen/einsicht/einsicht-07.pdf

Kay, A.J., 'Transition to Genocide, July 1941: Einsatzkommando 9 and the Annihilation of Soviet Jewry', *Holocaust and Genocide Studies*, 27, 3 (Winter 2013), pp.411-42

Kershaw, I., 'Improvised Genocide? The Emergence of the "Final Solution" in the "Warthegau"', in *Transactions of the Royal Historical Society*, 2 (Cambridge: Cambridge University Press, 1992), pp.51-78

Lasky, M.J., 'The First Glimmer of Extermination', in *Commentary*, 1 August 1948: https://www.commentarymagazine.com/articles/melvin-lasky/the-first-glimmer-of-exterminationplate-glass-pogrom-and-aftermath/

Lösener, B., 'Als Referent im Reichsministerium des Innern', in *Vierteljahrshefte für Zeitgeschichte*, 9, 3 (July 1961), pp.262-313

Lower, W., 'The History and Future of Holocaust Research', in *The Tablet*, 26 April 2018: https://www.tabletmag.com/jewish-arts-and-culture/culture-news/260677/history-future-holocaust-research

Michman, D., 'Täteraussagen und Geschichtswissenkraft – Der Fall Dieter Wisliceny und der Entscheidungsprozess zur "Endlösung"' in Matthäus, J. and Mallman, K.M. (eds), *Deutsche, Juden, Völkermord – Der Holocaust als Geschichte und Gegenwart* (Darmstadt: Wissenschaftliche Buchgesellschaft, 2006), pp.205-19; 'Perpetrator Testimony and Historiography: The Case of Dieter Wisliceny and the Decision-Making Process on the "Final Solution"', *Journal of Contemporary Antisemitism*, 1, 2 (Spring 2018), pp.15-32

Mommsen, H., 'National Socialism – Continuity and Change', in Laqueur, W. (ed.), *Fascism: A Reader's Guide: Analyses, Interpretations, Bibliography* (Berkeley, CA: University of California Press, 1976), pp179-210; 'Die Realisierung des Utopischen: Die "Endlösung der Judenfrage" im "Dritten Reich"', in *Geschichte und Gesellschaft*, 9, 3 (1983), pp.381-420; 'Hitler's Reichstag Speech of 30 January 1939', in *History and Memory*, 9, 1/2 (1997), pp.147-61

Musial, B., 'The Origins of "Operation Reinhard": The Decision-Making Process for the Mass Murder of the Jews in the *Generalgouvernment*', *Yad Vashem Studies*, XXVIII (2000)

Orth, K., 'Rudolf Höss und "Die Endlösung der Judenfrage" – Drei Argumente gegen deren Datierung auf den Sommer 1941', in *Werkstatt Geschichte* (1997) 18, pp.45-57

Pohl, D., 'Die grossen Zwangsarbeitslager der SS – und Polizeiführer Juden im Generalgouvernement 1942-1945' in U. Herbert, K. Orth and C. Dieckmann (eds), *Die Nationalsocialistischen Konzentrationslager – Entwicklung und Struktur*, I (Göttingen: Wallstein Verlag, 1998), pp.415-38

Poole, D.C., 'Light on Nazi Foreign Policy', in *Foreign Affairs* (October 1946), pp.130-54

Porat, D., The Holocaust in Lithuania – some unique aspects', in Cesarani, D. (ed.), *The Final Solution – origins and implementation* (London and New York: Routledge, 1994), pp.159-74: http://defendinghistory.com/wp-content/uploads/2011/09/Dina-Porats-The-Holocaust-in-Lithuania.pdf

Rothkirchen, L., 'Vatican Policy and the "Jewish Problem" in "Independent" Slovakia' (1939-1945) in Marrus, M. (ed.), *The Nazi Holocaust, Part 8 – Bystanders to the Holocaust*, 3 (Berlin: de Gruyter, 1989), pp.1306-32

Sandkühler, T., review of Florent Brayard's *Auschwitz, Enquête sur un Complot Nazi* (Paris: Seuil, 2012). Accessed on 16 February 2021 from: https://www.hsozkult.de/publicationreview/id/rezbuecher-18397

Schulte, J.E., 'Die Wannsee-Konferenz im Kontext von SS-Arbeitskräfteplanung und Völkermord 1941/42', Vortrag am 20 Januar 2003 im Haus der Wannsee-Konferenz, Berlin: https://www.ghwk.de/fileadmin/Redaktion/PDF/Jahrestage/2003-schulte.pdf

Snyder, T., 'Hitler's inevitable decision', in *History Today*, 12 December 2015

Stengers, J., 'Himmler et l'extermination de 30 millions de Slaves', in *Vingtième Siècle*, 71, 1 (2001), pp.3-11

Streim, A., 'The Tasks of the SS Einsatzgruppen', in The Simon Wiesenthal Center Annual, 4 (1987), pp.309-28: https://www.museumoftolerance.com/education/archives-and-reference-library/online-resources/simon-wisenthal-center-annual-volume-4/annual-4-chapter-9.html

Terry, N., 'Conflicting Signals: British Intelligence on the "Final Solution" through Radio Intercepts and Other Sources, 1941-1942', in *Yad Vashem Studies*, XXXII (2003), pp.351-96

Trevor-Roper, H., 'Nazi Bureaucrats and Jewish Leaders', in *Commentary*, 1 April 1962

Witte, P., 'Two Decisions Concerning the "Final Solution to the Jewish Question": Deportations to Lodz and Mass Murder in Chelmno', in *Holocaust and Genocide Studies*, 9, 3 (Winter 1995), pp.318-45

Wolin, R., 'The Banality of Evil – The Demise of a Legend', in *Jewish Review of Books* (Fall 2013): https://jewishreviewofbooks.com/articles/1106/the-banality-of-evil-the-demise-of-a-legend/

Yad Vashem Shoah Resource Centre, 'An interview with Prof. Christopher Browning' (March 1997): http://www.yadvashem.org/odot_pdf/Microsoft%20Word%20-%203848.pdf; 'An Interview with Prof. Hans Mommsen' (December 1997): http://www.yadvashem.org/odot_pdf/Microsoft%20Word%20-%203850.pdf

Index

Page numbers followed by an n indicate an endnote.

Ebert, Friedrich - 13, 16 n10
Eichholtz, D. - 103 n23, 118
Eichmann, Adolf - Austrian Jews, 19, 22 n11;
  Belzec, 57, 86-7; dating of Heydrich's
  'little speech', 95-99, 101; denials, 95-8;
  disappears, 31, 95, 103 n16; 'full powers',
  30-3, 39, 92, 94, 95; Globocnik and AE,
  86-7, 94-5, 99, 101; 'Himmler's
  specialist', 92; in charge of Nisko scheme,
  19, 54; Lodz negotiations, 52, 54, 60;
  organiser-in-chief, 20, 58, 61, 66, 86, 90
  n16; Riga, 53-5; Serbian Jews, 45; trial,
  31, 34 n8, 87, 96, 101, 102 n1, 103 n17,
  115; visits execution sites, 87, 88, 90 n11,
  103 n18; Wannsee conference, 66, 69-70
  n13, 81, 87, 88-9, 95, 101; Wisliceny on
  AE, 37, 93-6, 100, 101, 102 n12, 102-3
  n13, 103 n15, 103 n16, 121
Epstein, Catherine - 58 n4, 118
Erickson, John - 69 n2, 118
Evans, Richard J. - 102 n8, 114 n1, 118
extermination camps - 3, 104 n30, 113;
  Auschwitz, 83 n3, 88, 94, 97, 100, 104
  n38, 104 n40, 113, 118, 119, 122; Belzec,
  57, 86-7, 88, 90 n9, 99, 107; Chelmno, 50
  n6, 52-3, 87, 122; Treblinka, 100

Falls, Cyril -15, 118
Far East, the - 36
'Final Solution'(*Endlösung*)(see also:
  extermination camps, genocide,
  Holocaust and Jews) - 4, 5-6, 8, 9 n9, 9
  n18, 10 n26, 10 n32, 30, 33, 34 n15, 43 n8,
  50, 50 n6, 55, 58 n3, 63 n6, 66, 70 n17, 74,
  Chapter 11 *passim*, 86, 90 n15, 93-4, 98,
  100, 102, 102 n5, 103 n14, 103 n15, 110
  n3, 106, 111, 114, 118, 119, 120, 121, 122
Finland - 70
Fleming, Gerald - 5, 9 n18, 9 n19, 70 n17, 102
  n5, 118
France - 11, 12, 14, 17, 19, 20, 24, 28, 29, 44,
  46, 61, 62, 76, 78, 112
Frank, Hans - 3, 20, 52, 57, 66-7, 73, 74, 78-9,
  95, 99, 104 n31
Frank, Karl Hermann - 47-9
Fraser, Lindley -15, 118
Frick, Wilhelm - 92
Friedlander, Henry - 110 n14, 116
Friedländer, Saul - 9 n19, 121
Friedrichsruh - 104 n29
Fröhlich, Elke -28 n11, 42 n2, 43 n11, 43 n23,
  69 n5, 77 n3, 77 n15, 90 n19, 116
Funk, Walter -104

Galen, Clemens von - 38
General Gouvernement - 29, 45, 52, 54, 56, 59
  n16, 66, 73, 78, 81, 83 n13, 88, 90 n13, 90

n16, 99, 104 n30, 104 n39, 106, 113,
  119, 122
Geneva -108-9
genocide (see also: extermination camps,
  'Final Solution', Holocaust and Jews) - 3,
  7, 10 n22, 10 n24, 42 n5, 53, 58 n3, 103,
  106, 114 n4, 118, 120, 121
Gerlach, Christian - 6, 72-4, 77 n4, 83 n7, 90
  n11, 102 n3, 121
German Academy, the - 68
German Foreign Ministry - 22 n17, 27, 34 n4,
  44-5, 46, 61, 66, 79
German Interior Ministry - 39, 41, 52, 66, 78,
  80, 81, 83 n2, 92
German Ministry for the Occupied Eastern
  Territories - 24, 34 n4, 54-6, 66, 67, 74
German Ministry of Justice - 92
German Ministry of Labour - 60-1
German Propaganda Ministry - 3, 27, 39, 107,
  108, 109, 110, 121
Germany -Anti-Komintern Pact, 68; armed
  forces (*Wehrmacht*), 4, 11, 19, 24, 25, 36,
  37, 44, 47, 74, 75, 76, 78, 104 n33;
  launching of Operation Barbarossa, 21-
  22, 24, 112 ; collapse in 1918, 6, Chapter
  1 *passim*, 19, 20, 45, 48, 63, 76, 85, 114;
  declaration of war on the United States,
  71, 75, 113; defeat of France, 19, 29, 112;
  Hague Convention, 25, 27, 41, 44; Non-
  Aggression Pact with Soviet Union, 19;
  Treaty of Versailles, 12, 13; Tripartite
  Pact, 21, 71
Gerwarth, Robert - 51 n16, 118
Gestapo, the (the secret state police) - 18, 26,
  30, 31, 32, 38, 61, 81
Gilbert, Gustave - 9 n6, 9 n7, 116
Glass, Hildrun - 58 n8, 116
Globocnik, Odilo - 56-7, 59 n14, 59 n16, 66,
  86-7, 88, 91, 94-5, 97, 101, 107; invents
  own killing 'process' (Operation
  Reinhardt), 87, 90 n13, 90 n17, 91, 94-5,
  99-100, 101, 104 n30, 106, 107, 119
Glücks, Richard - 88, 94, 98
Goebbels, Joseph - 3, 7, 20, 22 n15, 28, 69
  n11, 32, 36, 42, 78, 110 n10, 113; diaries,
  6, 28 n11, 38, 42 n2, 43 n11, 43 n23, 69
  n5, 72, 75, 77 n3, 77 n15, 90 n19, 102
  n4, 106-7, 108, 110 n1, 116; deportation
  of Jews, 38-40, 45, 60, 62-3, 64, 65, 66,
  112; extermination, 68-9, 69 n9, 70
  n21, 76, 81, 85, 86, 90, 91, 106-9, 113,
  114; 'Jewish' war, 18, 21, 27-8, 28 n11,
  107, 108, 112, 121, 94; marking of
  Jews, 39, 41
Goering, Hermann -14, 16 n12, 16 n15, 24-5,
  27, 68, 92; appoints Heydrich to promote
  Jewish emigration, 18, 29; extends
  Heydrich's commission, 30, 32-3, 39, 79,